TO Kim

from
mom. 2013

Enjoy

Everything Else

STORIES OF LIFE, FAITH AND OUR WORLD

JACK WYMAN

Carpenter's Son Publishing

Published by Carpenter's Son Publishing, Franklin, Tennessee

Published in association with Larry Carpenter of Christian Book Services, LLC
www.christianbookservices.com

Author Photo by Olivia Wyman

Cover and Interior Layout Design by Suzanne Lawing

Printed in the United States of America

978-0-9883043-4-5

Acknowledgments

God has blessed me beyond measure. To Him be all glory and praise! I'm thankful for my family, who have meant so much, done so much and loved so much; my friends, who have encouraged and guided me along the way; Prison Fellowship, which gave me a deeper understanding of grace, mercy and forgiveness; the congregations of East Benton Community Church and Second Baptist Church in Maine; Hope Church in Connecticut, and Grace Heritage Community Church in Texas–through their love and support I learned to be a minister; all those who encouraged me to write; Andy Butcher, for his insightful edits; Suzanne Lawing, for designing a beautiful book; and Larry Carpenter of Carpenter's Son Publishing, for his wonderful help on this project and for giving me this opportunity.

For Beth.
Your abiding love has enriched, comforted and deepened my life
and has helped me to see and appreciate everything else.

"I've been reading Jack's stories and listening to his take on life and faith for years! He inspires, motivates, teaches, and challenges me in very simple yet profound ways. Jack has a special gift of being able to provide honest and hope-filled responses to the wrestling we all go through in the journey of life. I believe this collection of stories will refresh the spirit of anyone seeking to live out their faith in these challenging yet exciting times."

Tom Ingala, Pastor, Hope Church, East Hampton, Connecticut

"Jack's unique blend of biblical, historical, and political knowledge gives him the creativity to write enriching stories that touch your soul and encourage your mind. Jack's writing makes you want to live a better life."

Stephen Maroon, Director of Marketing, Export-Import Bank of the U.S., Washington, DC

Jack Wyman is brilliant! From his preaching abilities, to his knowledge of the Bible, to his political science acumen, to his gifted writing, he is simply wonderful. But when it comes to combining these diverse disciplines, and drawing from each of them with his insightful perspective, his brilliance turns to genius. You'll love every page of his Spirit-filled book.

Dr. Gerald R. Mitchell, Jr. Pastor, Pioneer Baptist Church, Norwalk, California

"Jack Wyman challenges all believers to rise up and think about our role here on earth as followers of Christ. A masterful storyteller who has changed lives for decades, Pastor Jack delivers truth! This book is a must-read for all believers."

Tammy Kling, Author, There's More to Life, *and* Freedom; *Founder, The Homeless Writers Project, Flower Mound, Texas*

"The first time I heard Jack Wyman preach at a little Baptist church in Maine almost forty years ago, I knew he was a gifted communicator. Whether delivering a sermon, lecturing in a college classroom, or participating in a political debate, Jack is passionate, engaging, articulate, and unflappable. He is an equally gifted writer whose thoughts are the result of careful research, reasoned thinking, and a steady moral and philosophical compass. These stories reflect that clear thinking and a commitment to what Bonhoeffer called "costly grace."

Bill Leonard, professional librarian, Thomaston, Maine

"Jack strikes a chord of authenticity with his writings and expresses thoughts so clearly and eloquently that they touch my soul. This book is a true gem and encouragement for the heart."

Dick Paulsen, justice advocate, Auburn, California

"In my lifetime I have heard hundreds speak (live or pre-recorded) and read the published words of thousands. Five, ten, twenty, thirty years later, I can count with ten searching fingers the individuals whose writings and orations reverberate beyond a moment and echo still: General Douglas MacArthur's "The Long Gray Line" speech at West Point and many by Churchill (e.g., "Their Finest Hour"), for example, that rouse the heart and rile the spirit while also changing the mind for years to come—no small task. It is in such rarified air that I perceive Jack Wyman. A brilliant thinker, a creative force—philosopher, political and presidential historian, pastor and preacher, educator and author—Jack is one of the finest communicators speaking today."

Blake Leath, PhD, Founder/CEO, Leath Group, Dallas, Texas

"Jack Wyman writes with courage, clarity, conviction and compassion. His knowledge of the scriptures combined with his grasp of history, biography and current events offer insights that inspire and encourage. Jack knows how to write and reading him is a delight."

Dave Conn, fundraising consultant, Tampa, Florida

"Jack Wyman is a master of the written word. In each of his stories he eloquently paints an intriguing and poignant portrait of an event or condition of humankind, illustrating the imperfections and limitations of man and human understanding. He then peels back the layers to reveal the purposes, actions and grace of our loving Heavenly Father as He works in the lives of faithful followers. Every story draws you in, captivates your imagination and uplifts your soul. I highly recommend this collection of Jack's works."

Kirk Lundblade, investment banker, Southlake, Texas

"I believe in Christianity as I believe that the sun has risen—not only because I see it but because by it I see everything else."
C.S. Lewis

Contents

"Genuine Christianity is a way of seeing and comprehending all reality."
CHARLES COLSON

America's Four Gods
Did the Devil Make God Do It?
Einstein's Unknown God
Everything Else
Doubting Darwin
Shine!
Stop and Think
Success
The Bishop and the Nun
The Glass House
The Roman Catholic Scandal
The Wide-Angle Lens

"You don't choose your family.
They are God's gift to you, as you are to them."
DESMOND TUTU

Fit to a T
God's Lullaby
A Lasting Legacy
Showing Up
The Farm
The Strength of Quietness
The Vows
Far Above Rubies

"He has also set eternity in the hearts of men."
ECCLESIASTES 3:11

$\mathscr{I}$ntroduction

C hristianity isn't just about one thing.
Christianity is about everything.

That's the point of this book.

Christianity is about prayer and believing the Bible and going to church. But it's about so much more than these things. Christianity is also about everything else.

Jesus Christ—and thus Christianity—embraces all of life. Christians must understand this, believe it, and live it. Yet we naturally struggle against the temptation to lower the sights of our faith and resign ourselves to a less glorious and more pedestrian vision. It's so hard for us to be anything more than routinely earthbound. We shed our blinders only with great difficulty—sometimes with fear. Yet, when we narrowly compartmentalize our faith instead of integrating it into every area of life, we rob ourselves of the excitement and joy of living for Jesus. To live for Christ, as the apostle Paul would tell us, is to live for him fully. And to live for Christ fully is to live for him everywhere and in everything.

How important our faith is to us—and the difference it makes—all depends on how we see it. Nothing matters more than this—and nothing changes us more.

When I was young and full of hope, my sister, knowing my lifelong fondness for quotations, shared with me a quote from C.S. Lewis. "I believe in Christianity as I believe the sun has risen," Lewis wrote, "not only because I see it but because by it I see everything else." I've never read a better nor more concise description of what it means to have a truly Christian view of the world. Years later my wife, Beth, gave me a framed copy of this quote for Christmas. It sits in my office as a reminder of my challenge to see all of life in the light of my Christian faith. I've endeavored to live by Lewis' observation. God has changed me in spite of my sometimes arrogant and stubborn self. I entered politics as a young idealist over the objections of my pastor and the fears of my mother—who thought I'd eventually get hurt. While I loved it and still view it as one of life's noblest callings, in time I came to recognize the limitations of politics in changing the world—and especially in changing the human heart.

Although my only brush with the law consisted of occasional traffic tickets, God placed me for a decade in one of the world's greatest prison ministries, Prison Fellowship. In working with prisoners and ex-prisoners and their families, and with some of the most selfless volunteers and staff I've ever met, God again showed me what it means to "see everything else" in the light of Christianity.

So many times I've felt like Jacob at Bethel: "Surely the Lord is in this place and I wasn't even aware of it!" (Genesis 28:16, NLT). It's the surprises that have always made the biggest difference. It never ceased to amaze me that I was invariably blessed by prisoners more than I ever blessed them. Another limited horizon was broadened.

Jesus revealed profound truth through simple stories, and the Bible itself is the greatest storybook ever written. In this book are stories about life, faith, and our world. They're stories about people–some famous, others unknown. Some of these folks are in the Bible. Others might live in your neighborhood. Some are kings and presidents, some are prophets and disciples, and some are athletes and soldiers. Others are just ordinary people discovering what it means to live in this world as it is.

These are stories about hope and despair, joy and sadness, triumph and tragedy. They are stories about love and longing, life and death, fear and courage, and about Heaven and Hell. They're about history, politics, and current events; about the Bible, theology, and the church.

For half a century I've rejoiced in my Christian faith. And, like the people I've written about—and perhaps like some of the people who read these stories—I've also doubted and wrestled with my faith. I've wrestled with vocation, disappointment, decisions, moves, family, death, tragedy, and purpose. I've struggled with the sovereignty of God and the great mystery of his will. I've experienced being unemployed with a wife and three small children to support. I've lost a close friend to death unexpectedly and said good-bye to a parent. I've seen my children make good decisions and bad. I've struggled with what it means to be a husband and a father—and I've reveled in grandparenthood.

> NONE OF THIS, OF COURSE, IS UNIQUE. YOU'VE STRUGGLED YOURSELF. NOR HAVE MY EXPERIENCES EXCEPTIONALLY QUALIFIED ME TO SHARE THIS BOOK—BUT THEY HAVE MADE ME WANT TO.

None of this, of course, is unique. You've struggled yourself. Nor have my experiences exceptionally qualified me to share this book—but they have made me want to.

Christian writing is no good if it's not redemptive. In writing about the real experiences of real people, whether sad or happy, I've attempted to bring a biblical perspective and to write about the relevance of Christianity to "everything else." I've tried to lift my own spiritual sights and those of my readers. And I've tried to write from the view of hope. As both a preacher and a politician, I've been forced to confront the human condition—together in all its joyful possibility and sad disillusionment.

Six decades of living will affect you. In many ways, I've got more doubts and questions. In other ways I've become more convicted and principled about what I believe, what it means, and why it matters. I've experienced a deepening concern for the direction and fidelity of the church and the condition of our country. And so I've written about these concerns.

In his famous sermon on Mars Hill, Paul told the men of Athens that their "Unknown God" was indeed the one and only God—the God who made Heaven and earth. Paul told this audience of intellectual philosophers, "For in him we live and move and exist" (Acts 17:28, NLT). I prefer the clear beauty of the Authorized Version:

"For in him we live, and move, and have our being…"

After all, it's one thing to "exist." It's quite another, it seems, to truly "have our being." These words perhaps come closer to an understanding of Paul's main point to the Athenians. Yes, God made us, but he wants us to do more than "exist." He wants us to be much more than simply religious. God wants us to live and to move—that is, to choose and think and reflect and meditate and love and care—and to fully and completely "have our being." He wants everything we are and do and believe to be "in him."

Paul believed that Christianity was not just true but that it defined the truth of "everything else" about life.

Jesus explicitly prayed to his Father that his followers would not seek to flee or abandon this world. Instead, Jesus prayed that we would live as we should while still fully engaged in this world. He asked his Father to make us holy and to guide us by the truth. And he prayed that you and I would come to understand more clearly and practically what this means. To know Jesus Christ—to desire to be his true follower—is not just to see him more clearly. It is, through Christ, to see everything else.

Chapter One: A View of the World

*"Genuine Christianity is a way of seeing
and comprehending all reality."*

CHARLES COLSON

*A*merica's Four Gods

A merican poet John Godfrey Saxe once wrote a poem entitled "The Blind
Men and the Elephant."

Saxe based his poem on an old fable told in India about

> *"six men of Indostan,*
> *to learning much inclined,*
> *who went to see the Elephant (though all of them were blind),*
> *that each by observation might satisfy his mind."*

As one might expect when six blind guys go to "see" a creature as large as
an elephant, there was some vigorous disagreement. As each one grasped a
part of the animal, he proclaimed that this was indeed the whole elephant.
Saxe concludes his delightfully profound poem with this verse:

> *"And so these men of Indostan*
> *Disputed loud and long,*
> *Each in his own opinion*
> *Exceeding stiff and strong,*
> *Though each was partly in the right,*
> *And all were in the wrong!"*

As Jesus sometimes did, Saxe then offered the moral of his poetic parable:

> *"So oft in theologic wars,*
> *The disputants, I ween,*
> *Rail on in utter ignorance*
> *Of what each other mean,*
> *And prate about an Elephant*
> *Not one of them has seen!"*[1]

I was reminded of this poem when I read a review of a recent book about God. Written by Baylor University sociologists Paul Froese and Christopher Bader, the book is entitled *America's Four Gods: What We Say About God—And What That Says About Us.*

While the authors point to surveys showing that nine out of ten Americans believe in God, the kind of God those questioned personally subscribe to varies greatly. Based on nationwide telephone questionnaires and more than two hundred in-depth interviews, the book identifies four quite different views of what God is like.

Some people believe in an authoritative God—one who judges human behavior and will punish it, perhaps through personal suffering and sometimes through natural disasters. From this perspective, AIDS and earthquakes are evidence of divine retribution. This God is a holy God who hates sin.

Some people believe in a benevolent God—one who is a direct and positive force for good in the world, less willing to condemn and more willing to forgive. This God is merciful and full of love and grace. This God doesn't send earthquakes to punish; he rescues and comforts those caught in them.

Some subscribe to the idea of a critical God—one who judges, but not here and now. This God will even the score in the hereafter. As in Christ's parable of Lazarus and the rich man, God will punish unbelief and injustice—and reward faith and meekness—after life is over.

Finally, there are those who believe in a distant God—one who, like a watchmaker, created the universe, started it going, and then left it alone. This God is the "Supreme Being" of America's founders. He is unknowable and mysterious but manifests himself through Nature. This God is the cosmic force of deism.

So who is he? Which is he?

In truth, God is all of the above. The scriptures reveal God to us in multiple dimensions of attributes and character. He is a God of judgment who is a "consuming fire." God will judge the earth. The book of Revelation teaches us nothing if not this. And God often intervenes in punishing sin and permitting the natural consequences of people's willful disobedience to his commands.

> IN TRUTH, GOD IS ALL OF THE ABOVE. THE SCRIPTURES REVEAL GOD TO US IN MULTIPLE DIMENSIONS OF ATTRIBUTES AND CHARACTER.

God is also a God of love. The Bible is replete with examples of his mercy and kindness. God's grace is the amazing theme of the entire Bible. Nothing proves the love of God any more powerfully than the greatest thing he ever did for humankind: giving up his Son as an atonement for our sins. God will also someday judge the "quick and the dead." One of the first activities of the afterlife is the Great White Throne Judgment.

Rewards as well as punishment are still ahead. God is also a mystery who cannot be fully known and who works in ways that are beyond our comprehension. God is "immortal, invisible...hid from our eyes," as the hymn writer notes.

Like the blind men of Indostan, we often grope for an understanding of God that is beyond our sight and beyond our grasp. There are not four Gods—there is only one.

This much is certain: "Our God Is an Awesome God!"

October, 2010

*D*id the Devil Make God Do It?

Y ou've got to hand it to Pat Robertson.

He really knows how to get attention.

The televangelist implied that the earthquake in Haiti in 2010 was the result of the ancient sins of the Haitian people. Robertson spoke on his program about how the Haitians, in order to win their freedom from the French in the 1700s, entered into some sort of "pact with the devil." While the Haitians won their independence, Robertson points to the country's long history of poverty and calamity—and its practice of voodoo—as evidence that God was displeased with Haiti for getting in league with Satan. Robertson believed the earthquake was just the latest example of this divine retribution.

Robertson, who drew immediate media coverage for his comments, has made it his consistent practice to attribute natural disasters to God's punishment for sin. He and the late Jerry Falwell famously claimed that 9/11 was caused by homosexuality and abortion. He made similar assertions after Hurricane Katrina.

We've speculated about the cause of suffering and the mystery of evil ever since the Garden of Eden. The Bible is filled with examples of God's judgment falling on nations and individuals because of sin. But simply claiming that every instance of natural disaster or other tragedy is the direct result of Satan's interference is probably giving the devil much more than his due. Satan may be the "prince of the power of the air," as the apostle Paul described him, and he is powerful. Yet as the old hymn says, "though the wrong seems oft so strong, God is the Ruler yet. This is my Father's world."

There are two reasons to reject the simplistic sin/catastrophe cause and effect in tragedies such as Haiti's earthquake.

First, the line between good and evil runs not through nations or cultures or political parties. That line runs through the heart of every one of us. Even through the heart of a televangelist.

When Jesus was told about the murder of the Galileans in the Temple, he surprised his listeners by saying, "Do you think those Galileans were worse sinners than all the other people from Galilee? Is that why they suffered? Not at all! And you will perish, too, unless you repent of your sins and turn to God" (Luke 13:2-3, NLT).

Jesus told us that instead of judging others, we should focus on clearing up our own vision and attitude. We must remove that beam from our own eye and judge our own heart first before we rush out to condemn others. In welcoming and forgiving the most notorious sinners, often quite publicly, Jesus offered an example of compassion rather than condemnation.

> IF WE PEER CAREFULLY THROUGH THE DEVASTATION, WE'LL SEE "THE POWER OF GOD" AT WORK EVEN IN HAITI,

Secondly, God works his divine will through tragedies—and even through sinful actions. He does this to glorify himself and rob the devil of satisfaction. When his brothers feared for their lives because of their treachery against him, Joseph reassured them. "You intended to harm me," he told them, "but God intended it all for good. He brought me to this position so I could save the lives of many people" (Genesis 50:20, NLT).

The disciples figured that the man born blind was that way because of his sin. Or was it perhaps his parents' sins? Jesus answered that it was neither. "This happened so the power of God could be seen in him" (John 9:3, NLT).

If we peer carefully through the devastation, we'll see "the power of God" at work even in Haiti, where faith in Christ, though tested in tragedy and suffering, has emerged stronger than ever through acts of courage and compassion.

Let's not give the devil credit for that. Let's give God the glory.

January, 2010

Einstein's Unknown God

In his biography of Albert Einstein, Walter Isaacson tells of a fascinating evening in Berlin in 1929, when a dinner guest, who had disparaged religion as a superstition, was informed by the host that Einstein, who was at the party with his wife, was himself a religious man.

"It isn't possible!" the cynical guest declared, and challenged the brilliant scientist to share his own views.

Einstein was calm and matter-of-fact in his reply.

"Yes," he confessed, "you can call it that. Try and penetrate with our limited means the secrets of nature and you will find that, behind all the discernible laws and connections, there remains something subtle, intangible and inexplicable. Veneration for this force beyond anything that we can comprehend is my religion. To that extent I am, in fact, religious."[2]

Einstein's brilliance, combined with his curiosity, forged a humble recognition and reverence for all that lay beyond his scientific discoveries. Throughout his life, it seems that Einstein's increased knowledge added to his deepening appreciation for the unknown—and the unknowable. It is ironic, perhaps, but understandable in the life of such a genius. The Bible tells us that only the fool has concluded that there is no God, and Einstein was no fool.

Isaacson claims that this change in Einstein's attitude was gradual and had taken a fuller bloom when he was about fifty. The author writes that "his beliefs seemed to arise from the sense of awe about the divine order that he discovered through his scientific work."[3]

Einstein did not believe in a personal God who intervened in the world. Nor did he subscribe to a hereafter ("One life is enough for me."). Einstein was a classic deist. But the great man revered the "spirit manifest in the laws of the universe" and he professed his confidence in a "God who reveals Himself in the lawful harmony of all that exists."[4] This may be contrasted with cosmologist Stephen Hawking's recent declaration that there is no God.

Einstein, one of the towering figures of the twentieth century, was not the first intelligent person to express his humble faith in a "force beyond anything we can comprehend."

"When I look at your heavens," declared the psalmist, "the work of your fingers, the moon and the stars, which you have set in place, what is man that you are mindful of him, and the son of man that you care for him?" (Psalm 8:3-4).

> "WHEN I LOOK AT YOUR HEAVENS," DECLARED THE PSALMIST, "THE WORK OF YOUR FINGERS, THE MOON AND THE STARS, WHICH YOU HAVE SET IN PLACE, WHAT IS MAN THAT YOU ARE MINDFUL OF HIM, AND THE SON OF MAN THAT YOU CARE FOR HIM?" (Ps. 8:3-4).

To the intellectuals gathered to hear him in Athens, the apostle Paul, himself a highly educated intellectual, offered some common ground amidst the secular skepticism:

"Men of Athens," he began, "I notice that you are very religious in every way, for as I was walking along I saw your many shrines. And one of your altars had this inscription on it: 'To an Unknown God.' This God, whom you worship without knowing, is the one I'm telling you about" (Acts 17:22, 23, NLT).

Paul then declared the truth about "the God who made the world and everything in it...the Lord of heaven and earth...He himself gives life and breath to everything, and he satisfies every need" (Acts 17:24, 25, NLT). This is Einstein's "spirit manifest in the laws of the universe."

"For in him," Paul said, "we live and move and exist" (Acts 17:28, NLT).

This is Einstein's "God who reveals Himself in the lawful harmony of all that exists."

This is the God who is "subtle, intangible and inexplicable," for the Bible declares "great is the mystery of godliness" (1 Timothy 3:16).

This is the God whom Einstein worshiped "without knowing."

Brilliantly, fascinatingly, and tragically, this is Einstein's unknown God.

This is the God Paul proclaimed. This is the God you and I can know.

September, 2010

*E*verything Else

I love quotes.

One of my favorites is from the twentieth-century Christian author C.S. Lewis. I often told my wife how much I enjoyed it; how profound its observations; how beautiful and simple its analogy. I quoted it so frequently that Beth decided to give me a framed copy for Christmas.

Here's what Lewis wrote:

> *"I believe in Christianity as I believe that the sun has risen—not only because I see it but because by it I see everything else."*[5]

The quote sits in my study, a continual reminder of the centrality and primacy of Christian faith. Lewis came to believe that Christianity either meant everything or it meant nothing. In his mind, there was no middle ground on the importance of faith. Christianity had to be both transcendent and pervasive. Faith in Jesus Christ had to invade every area of life. It had to be the lens through which we see the world. Christ had to be our eternal reference point. No matter what the interest, occupation, vocation, or subject, our relationship with Jesus has to inform it, guide it, and ultimately settle it.

The great danger—the perpetual temptation—for the believer is to relegate Christianity to a compartment of one's life. Christianity is then something one focuses on during Sunday mornings, enjoys, and then sets aside for the week. In the carefully compartmentalized life, Christian faith has no bearing on business, politics, finances, family, hobbies, ambitions, or various worldly pursuits. It is a part of life, perhaps even a fairly important part, but it has definite practical limits. In this view, Christ is important and helpful, but not paramount. We form our view on various things independent of Christianity.

The tragedy of compartmentalized faith is that it leads us to live as "practical atheists." We act and think no differently than anyone else. Faith is nice, it's attractive, but it is kept at a safe distance. It makes no lasting or profound difference on how we think or talk or behave.

We watch and cheer at the Super Bowl. We have our favorite team. We get upset when we don't agree with a call, become exasperated at missed opportunities. We are energized by the emotions we feel. We yell and we gesture. We eat our popcorn and our chips; we drink our soda and our beer. We end the game elated or disappointed.

But on Monday morning, there are very few of us who make any judgment or decision, or are affected in any of our relationships, by what happened in that game. After all, we sigh, "It's only a game." It may have riveted our attention for two or three hours the day before, but now it's over and this is real life. We forget it and we go on. "Maybe next year," we shrug.

This happens sometimes on Sunday mornings. We get excited, enthused. We clap, we jump, we laugh, maybe we sing. The music is loud and energetic; the message is dynamic and relevant. The whole affair is quite entertaining— perhaps even convicting.

And then it's over. And we leave. And perhaps before we are out of the parking lot, we are back in the world. The spiritual high we've just experienced is already fading. By Monday, it's a distant memory. By Wednesday, it never even happened.

> TO PERSEVERE IN THE FACE OF LIFE'S TEMPTATIONS AND DIFFICULTIES IS PART OF AN INTEGRATED FAITH.

Admittedly, this is a struggle we all face.

To persevere in the face of life's temptations and difficulties is part of an integrated faith. To set our "sights on the realities of heaven," as Paul told the Colossians (Col. 3:1, NLT), is the great challenge of understanding—of seeing—Christianity in the midst of all that appears earthbound.

We all need to pursue a higher view of God. Jesus told us to seek God's kingdom as the top priority of our lives. When we commit to doing this–in the study of God's Word and in prayer—then we will soon discover, as Lewis said, that in the light of revealed truth, there is a Christian way of seeing "everything else."

June, 2010

Doubting Darwin

Along with Abraham Lincoln, British statesman William Gladstone, and poet Edgar Allan Poe, Charles Darwin was born in 1809. Interestingly enough, Darwin and Lincoln were born on the same day, February 12.

We all know that Darwin wrote _On the Origin of Species_, postulating his famous theory of evolution. That seminal work marked the 150th anniversary of its publication in 2009. Most Christians have long despised Darwin and his theory, arguing that his chief contention that all species of life, including human, evolved over time from common ancestors, is a direct attack on God and the biblical account of creation. This emotion-laden tension reached a kind of apex in this country in 1925 when biology teacher John T. Scopes was put on trial for teaching evolution in his Tennessee classroom.

Scopes was defended by the famous trial lawyer Clarence Darrow, while the state's case was argued by the equally well-known evangelical politician and statesman William Jennings Bryan. The case drew national attention. While the state won, Bryan was so thoroughly ridiculed in the press for his mindless intransigence, that American fundamentalism was driven underground for the next half-century.

Public education eventually came to accept the teaching of evolution. This was accomplished with such absolute allegiance that we almost forget that

Darwin had a *theory* of how we all got here; a theory that, while broadly accepted as truth, has yet to be proven as such. In fact, many might be surprised at how many scholars and scientists today—some in the nation's finest Ivy League colleges—do not subscribe to the theory of evolution as a plausible explanation for the origin of the species.

Not being a scientist—and wishing sometimes that I'd paid more careful attention in biology class—I watch that beautiful BBC television series, *Planet Earth*, and I stand in awe of the wonder, the majesty, the complexity, the intricate balance, and the incredible detail of this planet. I do not reasonably understand how anyone could watch that production for any length of time and not come to believe in an amazingly creative creator. Only stubborn pride would seem to exclude such a possibility in any objective mind.

What's ironic is that naturalist David Attenborough, the narrator of *Planet Earth*, has more recently narrated, in honor of his bicentennial, a documentary on Charles Darwin and his evolutionary theory. Attenborough says that evolution "revolutionized the way we see the world."[6]

That's quite a claim. I wonder why sixteen hours of *Planet Earth* didn't revolutionize Attenborough's own thinking!

> THE PSALMIST NEVER GOT TO WATCH *PLANET EARTH* ON TELEVISION, JUST IN REAL LIFE. BUT THAT WAS APPARENTLY ENOUGH.

The psalmist never got to watch *Planet Earth* on television, just in real life. But that was apparently enough:

"When I look at the night sky and see the work of your fingers—the moon and the stars you set in place—what are mere mortals that you should think about them, human beings that you should care for them?" (Psalm 8:3, 4, NLT). David sums up his praise to God the creator with this tribute: "O Lord, our Lord, your majestic name fills the earth!" (vs. 9, NLT).

Life is not without irony:

Charles Darwin once studied at Cambridge to become an Anglican clergyman. Somewhere along the way, he lost his faith. But I wonder, when out on the deck of *HMS Beagle* at night, all alone, did he ever look at the stars and, in that moment, doubt his own theory?

July, 2009

Shine!

A.I.G.

It stands for American International Group. But it could equally mean Another example of Incompetence & Greed. The American people have been understandably outraged that a giant company managed so poorly that it needed a $170 billion taxpayer bailout could then turn around and award $165 million in bonuses to some of the very executives responsible for the mess.

And this as the cost for our nation's economic recovery topped one trillion dollars.

Big numbers. Big problems.

At the root of all this is considerable corruption and greed. And it just seems to spread. Our nation is suffering from an inversion of values, as if the price tags have all been switched. Integrity and decency and honesty are dismissed, while greed and success and wealth are pursued at any cost.

A long time ago the prophet Isaiah wrote about this: "The scoundrel's methods are wicked. He makes up evil schemes to destroy the poor with lies, even when the plea of the needy is just" (Isaiah 32:7, NIV). Does that ring a bell? It sounds as contemporary as Bernard Madoff, doesn't it? What would Isaiah say if he could observe Washington and Wall Street up close and personal?

"When little men cast long shadows," someone once said, "it means the sun is setting."

What can you and I do? We can't change the culture of our major institutions. They're too big and too powerful.

But we can live lives of integrity. We can be honest in all our personal dealings and we can be positive examples, in word and deed, in small matters as well as large. Each of us can make that kind of a difference. Each of us can exercise a stewardship of influence. Each of us can choose to light a candle rather than simply curse the darkness of a declining culture.

Yes, these are difficult days for our nation. Christians may sometimes feel like they are Puritans living in the midst of Babylon. But God intends for this to be our opportunity to shine, and the deeper the darkness, the brighter the light.

Isaiah didn't stop with a condemnation of the corrupt. In the following verse he offered the hope of integrity and character: "But the noble man makes noble plans, and by noble deeds he stands" (Isaiah 32:8, NIV).

> GOD INTENDS FOR THIS TO BE OUR OPPORTUNITY TO SHINE, AND THE DEEPER THE DARKNESS, THE BRIGHTER THE LIGHT.

The next time Congress decides to send someone some more bailout cash, perhaps our representatives will look at the image that graces our dollar bill. On the eve of his inauguration as our nation's first chief executive, George Washington remarked, "Integrity and firmness are all I can promise." He gave our nation much more, of course, but were it not for these virtues above all others, we might not have made it as a free republic.

Another very wise man once wrote:

"Let not mercy and truth forsake thee: bind them about thy neck; write them upon the table of thine heart. So shalt thou find favor and good understanding in the sight of God and man" (Proverbs 3:3, 4, KJV).

May God bless our nation and may he shed his grace upon our land and may God crown our good "with brotherhood, from sea to shining sea."

March, 2009

*S*top and Think

A re liberals smarter than conservatives?

That's the recent assertion by Satoshi Kanazawu, an evolutionary psychologist at the London School of Economics. He discovered that young adults who identify themselves as "very liberal" score an average of eleven points higher on IQ tests than those claiming to be "very conservative."

Kanazawu explains that this is because more intelligent people are "more open to new ideas." He adds that liberals, being smarter than conservatives, can be confident enough to abandon their ancient belief in God. It should be no surprise, then, that Kanazawu found that those with higher IQs are more likely to be atheists.[7]

Kanazawu's intelligent liberals also welcome the chance to pay taxes and support foreign aid. By such a definition, Congress should be a Mensa Society!

Kanazawu's study recalls Winston Churchill's observation on the subject: "If a man is not a liberal at twenty, he has no heart. And if he's not a conservative at forty, then he has no brain."

I've met some pretty intelligent atheists. They remind me of this irony: "The fool has said in his heart, 'There is no God'" (Psalm 53:1, KJV). Undoubtedly all true liberals pride themselves on being "open to new ideas."

The writer of Proverbs, a very intelligent man, wrote: "There is a path before each person that seems right, but it ends in death" (Proverbs 13:12, NLT). The apostle Paul, no slacker in the IQ department, wrote that the minds of those who had smugly abandoned their faith in God "became dark and confused. Claiming to be wise, they instead became utter fools" (Romans 1:21, 22, NLT).

One may suppose that this latest study will be more grist for the churning mills of ardent conservatives and liberals in our politically polarized climate.

It also seems there is something for Christians to remember: God has a very keen interest in the life of the mind.

When asked what the greatest commandment was, Jesus responded, "Love the Lord your God with all your heart, all your soul, and all your mind" (Matt. 22:37, NLT).

"All your mind."

> **GOD HAS A VERY KEEN INTEREST IN THE LIFE OF THE MIND.**

We love, serve, and worship God, not only with our hearts. We also do so with our minds; with our intelligence.

Thinking is hard work. It requires discipline and self-control. Sometimes it's not very much fun. Oftentimes it's dangerous and scary. Charles Colson, a thinking Christian's hero, remarked: "The church in America is five miles wide and five inches deep."[8]

In a world of information overload and schedules stretched tighter than pigskin across a barrel, we are always in danger of pursuing trivia. We run the risk of falling into superficiality: superficial faith, superficial politics, superficial worship, superficial thinking, and superficial living.

Paul told the Christians in Rome during a very difficult time that they must not "copy the behavior and customs of this world..." Instead, Paul admonished them, "let God transform you into a new person by changing the way you think" (Romans 12:2, NLT).

This is intellectual regeneration. It affects our whole view of the world and of life.

Paul warned Timothy of tough times ahead, and then told him, "But you should keep a clear mind in every situation" (2 Timothy 4:5, NLT). Paul instructed Titus, another young protégé, to "encourage the young men to live wisely" (Titus 2:6, NLT).

In other words: Stop and think!

Peter tells us "wherefore, gird up the loins of your mind" (1 Peter 1:13, KJV). What does that mean?

Stop and think.

Other translations cast Peter's words differently, but the meaning is the same.

"Prepare your minds for action" (NASB).

Stop and think.

"Be alert and think straight" (CEV).

Stop and think.

"So think clearly and exercise self-control" (NLT).

Don't let the world call your tune. Read a good book. Pay attention to current events. Consider an opposing opinion. Go deeper with Jesus.

Stop and think.

June, 2010

*S*uccess

We all want it. Most of us work hard to achieve it. To many, success is what matters in life.

Ambition is to be commended. So is hard work. We admire successful people; they are our inspiration, our heroes.

Jesus once told a story about a very wealthy and industrious businessman. He had a "fertile farm," according to the account in the gospel of Luke. The man made the very best of it. He worked hard and expected all his employees to do the same. And they did.

The result of all this hard work was success. The fields "produced fine crops."

The businessman was an excellent planner and an efficient manager. He was also a great visionary. We would admire him. He possessed all the personal qualities required for great achievement.

Listen to him strategize:

"He said to himself, 'What should I do? I don't have room for all my crops.' Then he said, 'I know! I'll tear down my barns and build bigger ones. Then I'll have room enough to store all my wheat and other goods'" (Luke 12:16-18, NLT).

The man planned a major expansion of his business to accommodate his growing success. He was bucking for Fortune 500 status. He figured that after all this hard work, he'd enjoy the fruits of his labor: "I'll sit back and say to myself, 'My friend, you have enough stored away for years to come. Now take it easy! Eat, drink, and be merry!'" (Luke 12:19, NLT).

Now, at this point, we might smile, nod our head, and say, "This guy's living the American Dream. Good for him." And we'd be right. When hard work leads to success, it's a great thing. Criticism of the wealthy is too often fueled by envy—which is stoked by politicians.

When God abruptly steps into this success story, we learn that it is not to condemn anything the successful man has done. He's been honest and he's worked hard to get where he is.

The problem lies in what's he hasn't done.

He's hasn't recognized God. He hasn't included God in his plans, his ambitions, his dreams—or his success. He hasn't factored God anywhere into his life.

He's left God out. Now his life is over. And he never saw it coming. Suddenly, the eternal trumps the temporal. God calls this man a fool and tells him that he will die that very night. Then Jesus makes his application:

> THE GREAT TEMPTATION IN SUCCESS—THE GREAT DECEPTION—IS TO MAKE US INDEPENDENT AND SELF-RELIANT.

"Yes, a person is a fool to store up earthly wealth but not have a rich relationship with God" (Luke 12:21, NLT).

Success and material wealth are great blessings. The great temptation in success—the great deception—is to make us independent and self-reliant. Success can lead us to be presumptuous. It can often seduce us into believing that we, ourselves, have achieved what God alone has done through us. We forget to praise God and to honor him with our success. We believe a bit too much in ourselves, not enough in Him. We even forget our mortality. We leave God out.

We can achieve all the success in the whole world, Jesus tells us, and still lose our own soul. This is the great danger of living only for today.

"Lord, remind me how brief my time on earth will be," the psalmist prays. "Remind me that my days are numbered… My only hope is in you" (Psalm 39: 4, 7, NLT).

You can't take any of it with you. The man in the story learned that too late. May God help us never to forget that where we're going matters a whole lot more than what we're leaving behind.

February, 2010

The Bishop and the Nun

No one would fault Bishop Thomas Olmsted for his sincere commitment to high moral principle.

The Catholic bishop of Phoenix acted according to his conscience and the teaching of his church when he kicked St. Joseph's Hospital in Phoenix out of the Roman Catholic Diocese.

What had the hospital done?

It had authorized the termination of a pregnancy.

The expectant mother suffered from severe pulmonary hypertension. Had she continued with the pregnancy, she might have died, leaving four other children without a mom. Sister Margaret McBride, a nun who has spent her life caring for the sick and needy, approved this single exception to the hospital's no-abortion policy. Bishop Olmsted also excommunicated her.

However, the hospital ignored the bishop and kept the sister on. The Catholic Health Association, a nationwide network of Catholic hospitals, stood behind St. Joseph's.

So what are we to make of this incident?

One could argue that religious authority—even within the most authoritative church on the planet—is not what it used to be. Catholics—like many young Protestant evangelicals—are increasingly finding their own way, apart from denominational dogma. There is a growing spiritual independence that is both refreshing and alarming, depending on how one sees the implications.

Then there is the issue of abortion itself. What St. Joseph's did stokes the ever-hot flames of that decades-old public debate. Yet it seems there is another observation that may be even more important.

We Christians, because of our fairly conservative and orthodox view of the world, sometimes find it easier to hold to our convictions than to display our compassion. We may be more easily inclined toward judgment than restoration. We may be more willing to stand and fight for righteousness than to exercise forgiveness.

Sometimes punishment seems a higher priority than mercy. And, of course, on occasion it is. We would do well to remember, however, that in the Bible God balances his holiness with his mercy. The psalmist tells us that "Mercy and truth are met together; righteousness and peace have kissed each other" (Psalm 85:10, KJV).

God is both holy and loving. He is both just and merciful. His entire plan of salvation is founded on these twin pillars of divine nature. No matter how we may react to what Sister McBride and St. Joseph's did to spare the life of this pregnant mother, we must never forget that you and I are the choicest recipients of God's extravagant mercy and grace. We deserved God's wrath; we have received his kindness. We deserved God's condemnation to an eternal hell; we have received his invitation to an eternal heaven.

We have been given much which we do not deserve—and spared so much that we do. How can we not be merciful?

Yes, these are strident and divisive and very emotional times. The moral foundations of civilization are crumbling. Yes, we must stand and fight for the faith once delivered to all the saints. We must defend a rigorous orthodoxy and subscribe to a muscular Christianity.

> LET US LEAVEN OUR ENTHUSIASM FOR PURITY WITH THE YEAST OF CHARITY.

Still, let us also recall the cry of the prophet, pleading to a holy God for his own nation: "And in your anger, remember your mercy" (Habbakuk 3:2, NLT).

Let us leaven our enthusiasm for purity with the yeast of charity. "Man may dismiss compassion from his heart," wrote William Cowper. "But God will never."

In a world that can be both brutal and harsh, let us live by the words of our Lord Jesus: "Blessed are the merciful, for they shall obtain mercy" (Matthew 5:7, KJV).

In the exercise of authority and discipline, every leader should remember the wise words of a wise man:

"Mercy and truth preserve the king: and his throne is upheld by mercy" (Proverbs 20:28).

April, 2011

_The Glass House

With the Obama Administration's decision not to enforce the Defense of Marriage Act, the anti-gay marriage activists have been up in arms.

Again.

It certainly should come as no big surprise that this president would take this position. The only surprise is that he didn't take it sooner. His Attorney General says that the federal law that defines marriage as between a man and a woman discriminates against gay people.

Of course it does. That's the reason it was enacted.

Those of us who agree with the moral and legal defense of marriage that this law makes won't change our minds about the definition of sacred union regardless of the president's disagreement. After all, no civil law can legislate personal morality. Nor can it change personal conviction.

The heart is beyond the reach of the law.

This is both our hope—and our despair.

Just as the repeal of a law will never cause anyone to agree with the morality of homosexual conduct, neither will the enforcement of any law dissuade homosexuals from embracing and practicing their lifestyle.

Let the debates resume. In the end, if we believe what the Bible tells us about these hastening days, our objections to homosexuality are akin to placing a single finger in the crumbling dike of western morality. The sound and the fury of our opposition signify nothing.

But in the midst of despair, there is always opportunity. When it comes to defining marriage, perhaps we Christians are focusing on the wrong thing. The definition is too narrow. We're fighting the wrong enemy.

Not long ago, when a guest speaker at an evangelical church in New York City asked the three hundred young Christians in the audience, "How many of you are pursuing purity?" about ten hands went up.

The divorce rate among professing evangelicals is around fifty percent—about what it is among nonbelievers.

It seems that in just about every issue of *Christianity Today,* there's an anonymous article about a guy struggling with Internet pornography. As a church pastor, I continue to be surprised and mystified by Christians who see nothing at all wrong with men and women living together outside the bonds of marriage.

When his fakery was exposed, the wizard in *The Wizard of Oz* cried, "Pay no attention to that man behind the curtain!"

Well, maybe we should. Because "gay marriage" is nothing more than a futile distraction to a church being strangled by a crisis of popular immorality.

Our churches, our youth leaders, and our pastors need to teach, not about the legal definition of marriage, but about its biblical definition. Marriage in God's eyes isn't just about gays getting married. It's about a lot more than that. It's about chastity, purity, and self-control. It's about faithfulness and respect. Marriage is about decency and doing the right thing.

> JUDGMENT BEGINS WITH US.

Marriage is about honor. Marriage is about commitment. And marriage today is about doing the unpopular thing—and not doing the accepted thing. The Bible doesn't tell us that judgment begins in culture or Congress or the courts. It doesn't tell us that it begins with homosexuals. The Scriptures tell us that judgment begins "in the house of God." It begins in the church.

Judgment begins with us. In Shakespeare's *Julius Caesar,* Cassius tells his friend:

> *"The fault, dear Brutus, is not in our stars,*
> *But in ourselves…"*

Jesus warned us about the hypocrisy lurking in every easy condemnation of another. He said:

"First get rid of the log in your own eye, then you will see well enough to deal with the speck in your friend's eye" (Matthew 7:5, NLT).

So, first, let's teach our own children the virtues of sexual purity. Let's rededicate ourselves to honoring the vows we first made because we believed in the sanctity of marriage. Let's resist the easy-out of divorce and commit to the hard work of saving our marriages.

Until we've done these things—until we've taught our children well and stood up boldly for the biblical ideal of marriage in all its sacred beauty—let's avoid throwing stones from our glass houses.

March, 2011

$\mathcal{T}$he Roman Catholic Scandal

Winston Churchill once said of Russia, "It is a riddle, wrapped in a mystery, inside an enigma."[9]

Much the same might be said of the leadership of the Roman Catholic Church. Especially for evangelical Protestants not raised in the church, the policies, pronouncements, and actions of the Vatican often seem shrouded in mystery and strangely out of touch with our modern world.

This enigmatic appearance has been more pronounced in recent times as the church staggers under the weight of the growing pedophile priest scandal. There doesn't seem to be an editorial board or a columnist anywhere that hasn't had an opinion about how Pope Benedict XVI is responding to the enveloping crisis. Defenders and detractors abound.

For Christians of all persuasions, there are a couple of observations that are worth acknowledging for added perspective.

First, the Roman Catholic Church is one of the last remaining global forces for traditional morality and human rights. The most recent pope before Benedict, John Paul II, partnered with Ronald Reagan to successfully liberate much of Eastern Europe, destabilize the Soviet Union, and win the Cold War. For this, among many other contributions, he is remembered as the greatest pope of the last half-century, and one of the greatest ever. The church also continues to be a stalwart and uncompromising champion of the rights of the unborn.

Secondly, not all of the criticisms are the "wounds of a faithful friend." Some are the attacks of anti-religion secularists who are gleefully pointing to yet another glaring example of the hypocrisy and corruption of organized religion. Instead of grieving over the diminished moral authority of the church, they welcome it.

There are some principles to remember in the midst of this scandal, and lessons illustrated by it—for Catholics and non-Catholics alike:

1. Avoid mounting high horses. There have been plenty of scandals within the evangelical community; certainly there have been enough to caution us against any sense of pride or self-righteousness. Jesus warned us not to judge and invited us to cast stones only if we qualified as sinless. His words must guide us now. Sin has infected us all, the whole human race, Protestant and Catholic.

2. Confession is good for the soul. The apostle John told us that if we confess our sins, God is faithful and just to forgive us and to cleanse us from all our unrighteousness. While this involves personal confession—an idea that any good Catholic understands—it also applies to the corporate body. It even applies to the Vatican as it responds to this scandal. Fully and publicly acknowledging, without reservation or condition, the sins of the church in this area is important and necessary. Dismissing this sordid and appalling international transgression as "petty gossip," as did a cardinal, is wrong and not helpful.

> WHEN GENUINE REPENTANCE TAKES PLACE, IT LEADS TO RECONCILIATION —WITH GOD AND WITH OUR VICTIMS AND WITH THEIR FAMILIES.

3. The victims matter. The lives of thousands of innocent children over several decades were horrifically shattered. Many will never fully recover. Jesus takes the side of "the least of these"—the poor, the dispossessed, the weak. Jesus loved the children, welcomed them into his arms, and condemned those who would cause them to stumble. We must never forget this. Neither should the Vatican.

4. Repentance is the only path to restoration. Repentance means being honest enough to confess our sins, humble enough to seek forgiveness, and sorry enough to change. When genuine repentance takes place, it leads to reconciliation—with God and with our victims and with their families. The Bible calls this restorative justice. Only then can moral authority within the church be restored and a new beginning offered by a merciful and gracious God.

While we watch, let us also look within. Let us realize that there, in our own hearts, no less than in Rome, our prayer must always be:

"Lord Jesus Christ, Son of God, be merciful to me, a sinner."

April, 2010

The Wide-Angle Lens

Do you see him?

He's sitting at the table in the corner, hunched over, and writing on a scroll. He is a small man with a prominent nose and intense, dark eyes. His craggy face is furrowed by the deep lines of persecution and hardship he has suffered since he gave his life to Christ.

The room is cold and damp because this is a prison. The man who writes is chained to a Roman guard.

Paul the apostle is writing a letter to his fellow Christians living in a small Roman colony called Philippi, in the province of Macedonia. They, like him, have suffered persecution for their faith in Jesus. Paul wants to encourage them. And so he writes.

In time Paul's letter of encouragement to the Philippians would make its way into the New Testament and become a source of comfort and strength to the Christian church through the centuries. The great apostle writes about many subjects in this letter, but always from the perspective of joy and gratitude. Paul offers his warmest encouragement as he sits in the midst of the harshest of conditions.

It's one of several beautiful ironies we discover in the Bible.

A brilliant and ambitious man is suddenly confronted by the mighty power of Christ while on his way to arrest Christians. That same power transforms Paul's brilliance into wisdom and his ambition into humility. He is imprisoned for preaching the same faith he once opposed with a fury. Having suffered so much for Jesus Christ and now finding himself chained to a soldier in a cell, Paul bursts forth on the written page with an irrepressible joy.

Most of us wouldn't have found this an occasion for praise and thanksgiving. Paul did. He explains why.

One of the most amazing passages of his letter to the Philippian believers is when he writes about his view of his imprisonment. Paul has this unusual capacity to take a step back from his immediate situation—no matter how difficult—and see the big picture of God's providential purpose for his life. He knows that the key issue is not what has happened to him. It's not his imprisonment. It's not his deprivation or his suffering. It's the cause of Christ and his Gospel that truly matters.

Read what Paul says:

"I want you to know, my dear brothers and sisters, that everything that has happened to me here has helped to spread the Good News. For everyone here, including the whole palace guard, knows I am in chains because of Christ. And because of my imprisonment, most of the believers here have gained confidence and boldly speak God's message without fear" (Philippians 1:12-14, NLT).

"Everything that has happened to me" has occurred in order that God may accomplish a much larger and more glorious and more lasting achievement. Paul never forgets this larger context. He never lets this thing be about him. He never permits himself to wallow in despair and self-pity. Paul chooses to think and to believe differently about his circumstances. He joyfully embraces another perspective.

Romans know the truth. Christians find their courage. And in this Paul rejoices – even in prison.

Paul celebrates despite the fact that some preachers are insincere and jealous and selfish in their motives for proclaiming the Gospel. "But that doesn't matter," Paul says. "Whether their motives are false or genuine, the message about Christ is being preached either way, so I rejoice.

And I will continue to rejoice" (Philippians 1:18, NLT).

Suppose you and I decided to more fully embrace Paul's positive perspective—every day, in every situation of our lives.

Suppose we decided to see life from a longer and larger view—God's view.

What if we took our pride and our hurts, and our easily wounded egos; and we gathered up our self-centered "needs," and our fears and paranoia—and surrendered them all to the greater good and glory of Jesus Christ and his Gospel? No matter what.

> **SUPPOSE WE DECIDED TO SEE LIFE FROM A LONGER AND LARGER VIEW— GOD'S VIEW.**

God wants to make this sizable difference in our hearts, in our minds, and in our lives. And when God makes this change in us, you and I will discover real joy—and in that joy rise above the circumstances of our lives.

Like Paul, God wants us to see life through a wide-angle lens.

February, 2012

Chapter Two: Family Ties

"You don't choose your family.
They are God's gift to you, as you are to them."

DESMOND TUTU

$\mathcal{F}$it to a T

She's a remarkable woman.

Her bright blue eyes still twinkle. Her smile is still warm. Her spirit is still strong.

My mom lives nearby with my sister and her family. At eighty-two, she is still beautiful—small, agile, and with lovely white hair. Though a bit frail now, she is physically quite healthy. My sister Truly does a great job keeping Mother looking nice and making sure she is very well cared for.

However, those of us who love her know that the light of her life inevitably softens with each passing day. That's because, like millions of older Americans, my mom suffers from Alzheimer's.

What's amazing is that Mother has retained her indomitable optimism and cheerful disposition. While there are moments of quiet solitude, even in a crowd, my mom is still a delight to be around.

Each Mother's Day, America salutes women everywhere. We especially commend—and give thanks for–our mothers. It's a good time to realize how great they are. How blessed we men are to have them. Women in this nation—who couldn't even vote until the end of the first quarter of the twentieth century—today enjoy an unprecedented degree of influence and leadership in American society.

Our nation is better because of it.

One of the first things I realized about the saint who gave me birth is that she had a "life verse." This is an evangelical tradition that has tended to go the way of the hymnal. But when I was a kid, it meant something important. A person selected a favorite verse from the Bible that would be a guide in his or her life.

My mother picked Isaiah 40:31:

"They that wait upon the Lord shall renew their strength. They shall mount up with wings as eagles. They shall run and not be weary and they shall walk and not faint" (KJV).

I can't remember when I decided that this was the perfect life verse for my mom.

I was barely born when my older sister, perfectly healthy at the age of two, contracted a rare and incurable disease that rendered her barely above a vegetative state for the remainder of her forty-four years. I wasn't there when my mom lost her twins. I was only twelve when our house burned down, sending my father—with severe burns—into the same hospital where my mom was recuperating from surgery.

There were plenty of lean years financially, too, while Dad worked hard and Mom made everything go further to feed a large family.

My mom lived and taught her faith. She took her kids to Sunday school and church every week. She did so alone; her husband stayed home. For years, my mother faithfully prayed for Dad to come back to the Lord. She encouraged us to do the same. God heard her prayers: my dad got up one Sunday morning and put on the suit my mom always pressed and hung out in the belief that God would someday work a miracle in his heart.

> MOM'S ENERGY AND ENTHUSIASM FOR LIFE SEEMED BOUNDLESS. IT WAS AS IF SHE COULD RUN AND NOT BECOME WEARY. SHE SEEMED TO WALK AND NEVER FAINT.

She never gave up hope. Through all the ups and downs of her active and interesting life—through all the sorrows, trials, and tears—I never once heard Mother complain. She waited upon God with a deep and unshakable faith—and God renewed her strength. In the midst of her hardships, she seemed to mount up with the wings of an eagle. Her unquenchable joy soared high above her circumstances.

Mom's energy and enthusiasm for life seemed boundless. It was as if she could run and not become weary. She seemed to walk and never faint.

Yes, Isaiah 40:31 was a life verse that fit Mom to a T. Looking back today, I realize she was its living, breathing embodiment. She claimed all its promises and God kept every one.

On Mother's Day—no, every day—let's take time to thank God for our mothers. Take time to thank God for the mothers of our children. Thank him for all that they have lived, all they have taught, and for all they have done.

Thank God for all that they mean to us.

May, 2011

$\mathcal{G}$od's Lullaby

I thought grandparents were a bit over the top.
Until I became one.

I really had no idea. A good friend warned me that my mind would "turn to mush." I guess that's what's happened because when I hold my little Ava in my arms and she looks at me curiously and then breaks out into an ear-to-ear grin and starts kicking her legs, my mind's as good as gone and my heart melts.

There's nothing quite like it in the whole world: I'm crazy about that little baby! I've got her picture on my cell phone and show her off to anyone who will take the time to look. When I stood in line at the store buying her first toys from Grampy, I told the other customers, the clerk, and anyone else within earshot that these items were for my granddaughter. Everyone nodded, smiled, and congratulated me.

Then it dawned on me: I was a typical grandparent! Yes, I even enjoy saying, "Here, take her, I think she's hungry—or perhaps tired. Whatever it is, I'm not having fun right at the moment, so you take her." Ha! It's just like they said it would be! Perfect!

Along with her parents, I sing songs to Ava. I carry her around in my arms and I sing to her. I guess you could say I delight in her. To me, she's the most precious, the most beautiful, and the most adorable baby on earth. And singing to her is part of the joy I take in holding her close.

Ava is surrounded on all sides by love and attention. She truly is a blessed child. And she has been such a blessing to us.

You and I are in the same situation as Ava. We too are blessed by constant love and attention. There is one who delights in us. Constantly. He rejoices over us. And yes, he even sings to us.

He is our God.

We often think of prophets as being pretty stern and strange guys. They rain down judgment and implore repentance. But once in a while, we see among them a soft side. They unveil a divine tenderness that reminds us that, as John wrote, "God is love." The prophet Zephaniah writes: "For the Lord your God is living among you. He is a mighty savior" (Zephaniah 3:17, NLT). The prophet declares the presence and the power of the Almighty.

And then Zephaniah shows us the heart behind the holiness:

"He will take delight in you with gladness. With his love, he will calm your fears. He will rejoice over you with joyful songs" (Zephaniah 3:17, NLT).

God sings to us!

Is that beautiful or what? This is a portrait of the God who is both strong and tender.

> IN THE MIDST OF OUR HUMANITY, IT'S COMFORTING TO KNOW THAT WHILE WE'VE CHANGED A LOT SINCE WE WORE DIAPERS, GOD'S LOVE FOR US REMAINS THE SAME.

God's love for us knows no limit. It is everlasting and unchanging. Paul told the Ephesians that the love of God was truly beyond human measurement. We could only try to imagine its true scope. And we'd fail at that. His love is so deep, so high, so long, so wide.

It's been a long time since we've been babies. Our softness has been roughed up some and our cuteness has weathered just a bit. We struggle, work, sweat, worry, cry, and laugh our way through life. We're not always adorable. But we're always human.

In the midst of our humanity, it's comforting to know that while we've changed a lot since we wore diapers, God's love for us remains the same. And just when we need it most, he picks us up in his strong arms and holds us close to himself. He whispers in our ear, "I love you. Don't be afraid."

And then he sings us a divine lullaby.

August, 2011

ᴀ Lasting Legacy

H e was a scared, skinny, nineteen-year-old kid far from home. On the other side of the world, in fact. His buddies were dying right and left, literally. It would later be said of him and his comrades who fought on this island, that "uncommon valor was a common virtue."

My dad landed with the Fourth Marine Division on Iwo Jima in February 1945. It would be some of the fiercest, bloodiest fighting of World War II.

Dad told me later, as he recounted his days in the Pacific, that he did pray, but that he never tried to bargain with God. His was no "foxhole conversion." In fact, he told God that if he spared his life, he would probably go right back to living the way he had lived before. It was an honest, straight-from-the-heart prayer. Dad made no promises to the Almighty, not even on the sands of Iwo Jima. Not because he was too proud—but because he was honest.

My dad later gave his life to Jesus Christ. And, although he had refused to barter for his life on Iwo, my father spent the rest of it making a difference. He worked hard as an aircraft machinist, raised a large family, and remained lovingly devoted to his sweetheart for more than sixty years.

He taught Sunday school, served on the deacon board and was chairman of the church board of trustees. Later on, he became involved in local politics, serving as deputy mayor and, with great pride and a sense of accomplishment, as the chair of the board of appeals for several years. And he never stopped being a Marine!

My dad was my hero. The greatest man I've ever known. He was larger than life. Hardly a day goes by when I don't think of him and miss his wise counsel and warm encouragement. When I consider this charter member of "The Greatest Generation," I'm reminded of the lyrics of the old Dan Fogelberg tribute to his own dad, who was a musician:

"The leader of the band is tired
And his eyes are growing old;
But his blood runs through my instrument
And his song is in my soul —
My life has been a poor attempt to imitate the man;
I'm just a living legacy of the Leader of the Band."

My dad left some big shoes to fill. His courage and heroism, his service to his church and community, and his steadfast devotion to his family and his Lord, are all part of the legacy he left me. In so many ways, my life has been a poor attempt to try and follow his example. He did things I'll never do. He endured hardships I'll never have to face. He made sacrifices I'll never have to make. He taught me what it meant to be a man. And then he showed me. From his deeds, even more than his words, I learned what a life of integrity was.

> FROM HIS DEEDS, EVEN MORE THAN HIS WORDS, I LEARNED WHAT A LIFE OF INTEGRITY WAS.

God has also blessed me with a godly father-in-law who has been a dear friend and wise counselor for nearly three decades; he is a man for whom I have the deepest respect and affection. A man of quiet strength and dignity, he too has modeled Christian virtue and manhood.

Proverbs tells us, "A good man leaveth an inheritance to his children's children" (Proverbs 13:22, KJV). On Father's Day, we celebrate what we have been given by our dads. And, as fathers, we dedicate ourselves anew to leaving a lasting legacy of godliness to our own children.

Let's celebrate. Remember. Give thanks. And, by God's grace, try and be a great dad. Your children will be blessed by your legacy.

June, 2009

$\mathcal{S}$howing Up

It was not convenient.

When my assistant reminded me it was time to leave, I was in the middle of several pressing projects. There was public testimony to prepare for hearings the next day, meetings to schedule, and calls to return.

But I left. The work would get done. Just not right now.

I had to drive thirty minutes to the small elementary school in our hometown. Beth had reminded me that morning: "This is important; it really means a lot. Don't be late."

So off I rushed. In the car, I thought to myself, "How important is this, really? I'm going to get to the school. Then find a seat in the crowd and, before you know it, it will all be over. Does this really matter? Is she even going to know I'm there? More to the point, will she ever remember?"

I got to the school auditorium for the concert just in time to see our daughter Suzanne, standing in the back row, singing her little heart out along with about sixty other kids. She didn't see me. I didn't hear her. And in about twelve minutes the whole thing was over.

I hugged Suzanne and told her she did a great job. "Daddy's proud of you, sweetheart." She smiled and then was off to see her friends. I kissed Beth good-bye, she thanked me for coming, and back to work I went.

As I thought about being at that little concert, I realized that maybe I was wrong to dismiss it so lightly. It may have been a brief gesture of support, more symbolic of my role as a dutiful dad. But my wife knew I was there and that meant a lot to her. It was important for Beth to know that when the push of fatherhood came to the shove of work, I'd set the right priority and make the right call. I suddenly realized that those twelve minutes made a difference.

A man's work is important to him. One of the great hidden dangers of a job you love is that it spreads over your time like St Augustine grass—tentacles of demands shooting first this way and then that until, before you know it, it's taken over the lawn of your life. Family time suffers and even when you're with your kids, your attention isn't. Suddenly you're consumed by the wrong priorities. You find yourself investing nearly all your waking time and energy in the activities and achievements for which your kids will never remember you.

That's why, when it comes to your family, making time, even for seemingly small and simple things, is a very big deal. Attending a children's program or sporting event may not change the world, but it will change yours. And it will change your child's world more than you would ever imagine.

> WHEN IT COMES TO YOUR FAMILY, MAKING TIME, EVEN FOR SEEMINGLY SMALL AND SIMPLE THINGS, IS A VERY BIG DEAL.

Woody Allen is in the quotation books for saying one significant, wise, and memorable thing:

"Eighty-five percent of life is simply showing up."

The apostle Paul put the same wisdom a bit differently:

"Don't look out only for your own interests, but take an interest in others, too" (Philippians 2:4, NLT).

In no area of life is the application of this wisdom any more important than when it comes to our children. Showing up and taking an interest—being there for your kids—to encourage, to cheer, to applaud, to take notice and to take pride is the most powerful and life-changing thing you can ever do—for yourself and for them.

My three girls are young women now and I'm a grandfather. If I could go back and change anything—if I could make them all seven again—I'd pour a lot more of myself into them.

Just a few years ago, one of my daughters said to me: "Dad, one of the things I remember is that you always came to see me at school events. You were always there, no matter what it was."

Showing up: it makes all the difference.

June, 2011

The Farm

The farm.

When I hear those two words, my mind is flooded with a thousand warm and precious memories. My parents bought the farm in the summer of 1970, when they moved from Connecticut back to their native Maine.

It was there that I lived while going to college. It was there that I worked summers gathering hay. It was on the farm that I first met my wife, Beth. And the farm is where we brought our three girls to visit Grampy and Grammy Wyman. Each December, we picked out a Christmas tree on the farm.

There were a lot of meals with family and friends, a lot of laughter, a lot of living. Yes, a lot of great times on the old farm. I didn't want them to end. I figured they never would. I was wrong.

Today the farm that once was filled with the joys of simple life stands silent and empty. There's a For Sale sign out front. My father is now with the Lord. My mother lives with my sister here in Texas. For thirty-seven years the farm was a dear old friend, always welcoming us home. Today it's a memory, the inevitable result of change. The memories live on, and life moves on.

Change is the one constant of our lives and time is a relentless taskmaster. Perhaps the wisest words ever penned were, "This too shall pass." They are a comfort in the bad times—and a warning in the good. The older I get, the more I appreciate time. It is a restless river running through the middle of our brief lives. It is a rebuke to our presumption.

Nothing ever stays the same.

We change as people. We get older, hopefully wiser. Our kids grow up and leave home and have kids of their own. Our loved ones die.

We change as a culture, as a society, as a planet. We all grew up in a time when the world was simpler, more innocent, and less expensive. But that's true of every generation.

In the midst of continual change, we may draw comfort from the one who doesn't.

"I am the Lord," God says through the prophet Malachi. "I change not" (Malachi 3:6). James reminds us that "God our Father...never changes or casts a shifting shadow" (James 1:17). And the writer of Hebrews tells us that "Jesus Christ is the same yesterday, today, and forever" (Hebrews 13:8).

Most everything else does, but God doesn't.

> IN THE MIDST OF CONTINUAL CHANGE, WE MAY DRAW COMFORT FROM THE ONE WHO DOESN'T.

This means that the God who led Abraham out of Ur and gave him a promise is the exact same God who keeps his promises to us today.

It means that the God who spoke to Moses from a burning bush and commissioned him to lead a nation from bondage is the exact same God who answers our prayers and can work miracles in our lives today.

God will never change—he never grows weary or old. What does this mean to us? It means that God is also able to keep us and guide us and protect us today just as surely as he did when he walked in the fiery furnace with the three young Hebrews and shut the mouths of the lions before they could have dinner with Daniel.

The Bible that speaks with beauty and eloquence of our mortality says of God, "He is the Rock, his work is perfect" (Deuteronomy 32:4).

Times change. Old farms go up for sale.

But the God who loves us and sent his Son to be our savior is the eternal God, and underneath all the shifting sands of time are his everlasting arms, holding us and caring for us—forever.

He'll never change.

July, 2009

_The Strength of Quietness

He sat there contented.

He was quiet and relaxed. He didn't say a whole lot, but he was clearly enjoying the attention. He read his cards out loud in a soft but distinct voice. He smiled gently.

My father-in-law, Mr. Dale Kelly, was the guest of honor at the celebration of his eightieth birthday.

As those who love him most gathered to salute him, I again thought of what an extraordinary man he is and how very blessed I am to know him. He is my relative by law and brother in Christ by faith. He is my dear friend by choice. The advancement of years has neither dimmed his keen intelligence nor hindered his conversation. His walk-in-the-park gait has slowed only a little. A track and fielder in high school, Dale still visits the fitness center several times a week. He and Gaye still sing in the church choir.

In the loquacious home of my youth, if you didn't talk it meant you were upset. Silence was usually an ominous sign. So it took me a while to warm up to Dale. Or, more precisely, it took me a while to be reassured he had indeed warmed up to me.

Although a native of St. Louis, he shares the New Englander's economy of speech. I'll never forget my first visit to his home. I was dating his youngest child and felt the nervous urge to make a good impression. As I sat in the kitchen on the morning of my second day, Dale walked in and barely acknowledged me. He stood there scanning the newspaper.

Mustering all my courage, I rose, went over to him, and said, "Beth and I thought we'd visit Canton today."

"Well," Dale said to me, not taking his eyes off the paper, "good-bye."

I was crestfallen, figuring I was striking out. In fact, that was just Dale being Dale. It remains one of the family's favorite all-knowing stories. When I later heard that he had told his daughter that she was "getting a prince," I thought I'd won the lottery. He never told me that, but knowing that he believed it was a rare trophy. When I got a compliment from Dale, I knew I'd earned it.

Over the past thirty-plus years, I've discovered you have to prime the pump just a little to begin to tap the depth of Dale Kelly's still waters. But it's always worth the initiative. From geography to history to biography, and from art and literature to music and theology, Dale's knowledge and interests are broad and captivating. Like many quiet people, Dale is an engaging and thoughtful conversationalist.

He doesn't gush over. I've never seen Dale lose his temper, raise his voice, insist on his own way, or act rudely toward anyone—ever.

Dale isn't just a devout Christian. He's a man of consistent Christlike character and profound godly wisdom. He has loved his family, his church, and his God with a steady and unswerving devotion. His family means everything to him. So does his faith. While he's a man of emotional reserve— I've never seen him cry or heard him laugh out loud—his love and loyalty and sensitivity to others are as great as anyone I've ever known.

> DALE ISN'T JUST A DEVOUT CHRISTIAN. HE'S A MAN OF CONSISTENT CHRISTLIKE CHARACTER AND PROFOUND GODLY WISDOM.

As I've watched Dale slip gracefully into his sunset years, I've continued to rejoice in his uncompromised integrity. In an age when we see moral disappointment and failure all around—soaring egos, selfish motives, duplicitous conduct—what a stalwart example Dale has been to my family and to me.

Paul lists the qualities of temperament and character to which every Christian should aspire. In his letter to the Galatians, he calls them "the fruit of the Spirit." We sometimes hasten past them. Yet they comprise the mosaic of the Christlike portrait: love, joy, peace, patience, kindness, goodness, faithfulness, gentleness and self-control (Galatians 5:22-23, NLT).

Had I never known Dale Kelly, I might have been tempted to think that no mortal could possess all of these spiritual attributes. But in his daily life I have seen them, and so I know that, by God's grace, they are possible.

The prophet Isaiah tells us that "in quietness and trust is your strength"(Isaiah 30:15).

Dale Kelly has lived the truth of those words.

December, 2011

The Vows

S ummer is a special season.

School's out, vacations are on, and graduations are held.

And then there's something else that traditionally takes place in the summer: people get married.

Weddings are planned, rehearsals are scheduled, money is spent. People, most of them young, officially pledge their lives to each other. Weddings are glorious events. Some folks are nervous, but everyone is happy. Weddings are joyous celebrations of what has been called "The Greatest Thing in the World."

Love.

It brings men and women together. And at weddings, these young people earnestly promise that their love will keep them together "till death us do part." What that used to mean is that one person would someday escort the other to the cemetery. When asked if she ever contemplated divorce, Ruth Graham, Billy's saintly but lively wife, famously replied, "Never. Murder maybe, but never divorce."

Of course, attitudes toward both marriage and divorce have gone through quite a transformation over the past half century. The ancient vows aren't what they used to be.

Recently I was given the honor of performing the wedding of my niece Mary. She and her fiance, Ryan, make a great couple. I'm thankful God has brought them together and I pray He will keep them together—for the rest of their lives on this earth. And I'm gratified that Uncle Jack was trusted enough to officiate.

This is especially so because thirty years previously, I also performed Mary's parents' wedding. My sister Truly and her husband, Bill, made the exact same commitments to each other that their daughter Mary made to Ryan. With the same words they took the same vows. And, just like Mary and Ryan, they did that "in the sight of God and in the face of this company." Three decades earlier, Bill and Truly were filled with the same excitement, hope, devotion, and love that would fill the hearts of their daughter and future son-in-law.

The intervening years haven't been without their share of pain and sorrow or difficulty. No one's marriage ever is. Bill and Truly lost Samuel at birth. Their second beloved son, Zeke, now a teenager, is autistic. God also blessed them with both Mary and Abby. Bill and Truly worked hard, suffered their heartaches in each other's arms, and loved and trusted God—and each other—through all the ups and downs of their life together. Today their love is richer and purer and deeper even than it was thirty years ago.

> OUR LOVE IN MARRIAGE MUST BE ROOTED AND GROUNDED IN A COMMITMENT THAT TRANSCENDS WHAT HAPPENS.

It has always seemed to me somewhat ironic that the traditional wedding vows, recited in the midst of so much joyful anticipation, also speak of such things as "for poorer," "in sickness," and "for worse." It is perhaps to remind everyone present that the lives of these newlyweds are still uncertain and that they should not only look forward to great joy but also be prepared to weather some adversity. Just as God's love for us is not conditioned upon the unforeseen circumstances of our lives nor the changing feelings of our hearts, our love in marriage must be rooted and grounded in a commitment that transcends what happens.

Over the years, as I've seen marriages torn apart by infidelity, abuse, and the tragedy of lost love, God has taught me a greater understanding and appreciation for the desperate sadness that leads to divorce. And God has also shown me the hope and joy that can come with second chances and new devotions. So while my convictions have remained, my own heart has been made more tender by the heartbreaks of others.

"Love is patient and kind," Paul tells us. "It does not demand its own way... Love never gives up, never loses faith, is always hopeful, and endures through every circumstance" (1 Corinthians 13:4,7, NLT).

That's the love that has kept Mary's parents together.

It's the love I wish for their daughter.

July, 2011

$\mathcal{F}$ar Above Rubies

In the City of London, England, the Barnet Council has issued a strict twelve-page guide to its staff on the subjects of equality and diversity. Among the council's bans: no more mother-in-law jokes.

Such jokes are considered "offensively sexist" and disrespectful to "family elders."

Good luck with that.

Mother-in-law jokes have been around forever. In the first century, Roman poet Juvenal wrote a satire in which he said: "It is impossible to be happy while one's mother-in-law is still alive."

In the eighteenth century, Voltaire observed that "Behind every successful man stands a surprised mother-in-law." In the nineteenth century, humorist Josh Billings advised, "Be kind to your mother-in-law, but pay for her board at a nice hotel." More recently, someone pointed out that "Everything has its drawbacks—as the man said when his mother-in-law died, and they came down on him for the funeral expenses."

We all know the jokes. Sons-in-law have been telling them for centuries. But why have so many described a "pleasure trip" as taking one's mother-in-law to the airport? Why do these ladies get such a bad rap—albeit a gently humorous one?

It's true that when you marry, you don't just marry your spouse—you also marry into their family. And that cast of characters isn't always the one we'd choose if all other things were equal. Of all the in-laws one gains with marriage, arguably the most challenging is the mother-in-law. She's often skeptical, sometimes critical, and occasionally intrusive. She's usually blindly loyal and excessively protective—toward her daughter (or son). She can also be the master of gratuitous advice.

The mother-in-law is the other "significant other" in a married person's life.

Gaye Kelly at this point would say, "Yes, Jack, and you'd be wise to remember that." She'd have a momentary serious look. Then she'd smile and softly chuckle. Billie Gaye, as she was named when she was born eighty years ago in the tiny west Texas town of Electra, has been my mother-in-law for more than thirty years. While she's had to adjust to her family's first New Englander, it might also be said that when it comes to the popular perceptions, Gaye has been an atypical mother-in-law.

Sure, she poked good-natured fun at my pronunciation of "butta" at our first dinner, but Gaye has truly been one of my most loyal and enduring fans. Her gentle spirit and gracious manner have never—on any occasion —failed her. Her five children have attempted to persuade me that Gaye's mellowed out considerably since their childhood. I've always rejected that notion—which, of course, she'd expect me to.

If Gaye's had opinions—and I'm sure she has—she's always been discreet. Although she is the one person outside our marriage who my wife Beth would go to in a crisis—for advice or just to listen—Gaye has never come to me with her own counsel. She has never interfered. In this, Gaye has managed to be a loving and supportive mother without being a meddlesome mother-in-law. That's no small task.

When we lived in New England, the ride to the airport after one of Gaye's visits was hardly a "pleasure trip." It was sad to say good-bye and there were always moist eyes. After our girls were born, ending the visits was a bit harder. It was

> HER WEST TEXAS BLOOD COURSES THROUGH THE VEINS OF OUR DAUGHTERS AND I TAKE PRIDE IN THAT. I PRAY THAT THEY WILL BE LIKE HER—AND LIKE HER DAUGHTER.

only after we moved to Texas that I discovered that Gaye—one of the most devout Christians I've ever known—had been praying for years that God might open the door for a relocation. Beth didn't even know. Not once over all those years was there ever a complaint or even a strategically planted regret. But there was plenty of joy when God finally answered Gaye's secret prayer.

Her hair has turned a beautiful snow-white as she has slipped gracefully into senior citizenship. Her mind is clear and her gentle wit remains intact. Her love for God and for her family continues to be her quiet passion. Her west Texas blood courses through the veins of our daughters and I take pride in that. I pray that they will be like her—and like her daughter.

It's difficult for me to read about the "virtuous woman" described in Proverbs 31 and not to think of Gaye Kelly—"for her price is far above rubies." I, of all sons-in-law, am most richly blessed.

May, 2012

Chapter Three: Caesar's Household

"All the saints send you greetings, especially those who belong to Caesar's household."

PHILIPPIANS 4:22, NIV

"Is there no virtue among us? If there be not...no form of government can render us secure."

JAMES MADISON

*C*areful Wish

Be careful what you wish for.
It's old advice. It's wise advice.

Christians want a president who believes like they do. So the candidates have been pouring faith on their politics like catsup on a hotdog—trying to outdo each other to become "Pastor-in-Chief." Interestingly, the candidates most overt about their personal faith are no longer in the race. This doesn't stop the faithful from pining for one of their own in the White House. In South Carolina, where born-again Christians did not support him—and perhaps in other states—Mitt Romney's devout Mormonism may still be an issue for some evangelicals.

The desire to have more religion in our politics, however, should be tempered by a thoughtful consideration of the power of the State.

In New York City, the U.S. Second Court of Appeals has told churches they cannot hold a "religious worship service" in a public school building after school hours. The Obama Administration has also stirred controversy by ordering the Catholic Church and other religious institutions that serve the general public to provide contraceptives, sterilization, and abortion-inducing drugs to employees—in violation of their religious convictions.

As Christians see this government encroachment upon faith, it is understandable that we would seek a redress of our grievances through the election of more Christians to public office.

We should be careful.

Quite apart from the constitutional prohibition against any religious test for holding public office and the transparent manipulation of Christian leaders by politicians seeking their support, there is the question of power itself.

Shortly after he assumed the presidency in the summer of 1974, following the greatest constitutional crisis and abuse of power in American history, Gerald Ford spoke to a joint session of Congress and summarized the lesson of the crisis:

"A government big enough to give you everything you want is a government big enough to take from you everything you have."

This is an axiom of power that we ignore at our peril.

When the Roman emperor Constantine became a Christian in the fourth century, he ended the persecution of believers and ushered in a period of religious toleration. He appointed Christians to high office. Christians rejoiced—for a while. But eventually, Constantine began to look to other deities, such as Diana and Apollo and Hercules. This led, in time, to the emperor ordering both Christians and non-Christians to join in worshiping the sun.

The State and the church had united—and, in the end, Christianity was the loser.

In his new biography of the New England Puritan Roger Williams, *Roger Williams and the Creation of the American Soul,* John M. Barry points out that Williams rebelled not against the theology of the colonial government, which he shared, but its coercive power. Long before Jefferson did, Williams advocated that there be a "hedge or wall of

> WILLIAMS BELIEVED THAT IT WAS MORE IMPORTANT TO PROTECT THE CHURCH FROM THE STATE THAN THE STATE FROM THE CHURCH.

Separation between the Garden of the Church and the Wilderness of the world."[10]

In this, Williams believed that it was more important to protect the church from the state than the state from the church.

Israel was not content to have God as its ruler. It wanted a king. The prophet Samuel warned the people of the dangers of secular power, but they paid no heed. So they got their king: Saul, whose life and reign was a tragedy—for him, his family, and for the nation.

The psalmist tells us: "Put not your trust in princes, nor in the son of man, in whom there is no help" (Psalm 146:3, KJV).

"Some trust in chariots, and some in horses: but we will remember the name of the Lord our God," declares David in the twentieth Psalm (20:7, KJV).

"Government is not reason, nor eloquence," wrote George Washington. "It is force. And like fire, it is a dangerous servant and a fearsome master."

That's advice worth pondering—offered by a man who wisely understood the dangers and temptations of power.

As we move through this presidential campaign and listen to the claims and counter-claims of those who would lead us, when it comes to the combustible combination of religion and politics, we should employ a healthy skepticism.

And we'd best be careful for what we wish.

February, 2012

Storms

They've packed up and left town.

They've taken down their banners, swept up their confetti, and filed away their speeches. The two great national political conventions of 2012 are now history. They were held back–to-back in the late summer of last year. The Republicans convened in Tampa; the next week, the Democrats gathered in Charlotte. Through all the rhetoric and hoopla, each convention strived to convince Americans watching at home why the other party couldn't be trusted and why their guy was the one to put things right.

With polls showing America deeply divided, it seemed as if we were observing alternative universes in Charlotte and Tampa—two competing visions and two widely diverse interpretations of our problems, their causes, and their remedies. Then their champions sallied forth across the country warning of Armageddon and promising the Moon. One is tempted to paraphrase the ancient liturgy: "as it was in the beginning, so it is now and ever shall be—world without end: Democrats and Republicans!"

"There's nothing as shortsighted as a politician," cracked Will Rogers, "unless it's a delegation of them."

Or perhaps a convention. In any event, they were harmless fun to watch. What did these two national political gatherings have in common? The weather, it turned out.

The Republicans decided to delay their convention a day because of the threatening path of tropical storm Isaac. A week later, the Democrats moved their final event—the president's acceptance speech—from a 74,000–seat outdoor football stadium into a 20,000-seat indoor basketball arena because of approaching severe thunderstorms.

In both cases, high winds, heavy rain, and bolts of lightning altered the best-laid plans of those who would presume to chart the course of the world. The elements of nature forced the most powerful man on earth—who four years ago stood outdoors between faux Greek columns—to seek cover inside. Everyone was disappointed but powerless to stop it. Even Bill Clinton's soaring eloquence was not enough to open the sunrays of heaven.

Were I Pat Robertson, I might be tempted to suggest that a provoked God had hurled down his vengeful lightning upon a party that had at first removed his name from their platform, only to have second thoughts and re-insert it. That would be fun to argue. Yet, as we approached the most important decision we collectively made as a free people, choosing a president, it would have been wise to see these unwelcome meteorological events not as a recrimination but as a reminder.

> GOD IS NEITHER A REPUBLICAN NOR A DEMOCRAT. THOUGH OFTEN INVOKED, HE IS HARDLY A MASCOT. HE IS NEITHER THE CHAMPION OF PARTISAN CAUSES NOR THE DEFENDER OF POLITICAL PLATFORMS. GOD'S NOT EVEN AN AMERICAN.

God is neither a Republican nor a Democrat. Though often invoked, he is hardly a mascot. He is neither the champion of partisan causes nor the defender of political platforms.

God's not even an American.

God is nobody's campaign manager and he was not crossing his divine fingers on the outcome of this election. Instead, God reigns supreme over the events of people and nations. His plan for America will in no way be thwarted by the electoral outcome. It is an outcome that he both knew and had ordained. When we fret and worry and fight, we show that we have placed our faith in campaigns and the promises of politicians and not in the Creator of the heavens.

It has been well said that "Man proposes but God disposes." When Napoleon in arrogance tried both, he discovered that the military baton was no match for the scepter of the Almighty—as did Hitler, when he too left his army frozen in the Russian winter. Man may shake his fist in the face of God or seek the divine stamp upon his own ambitions, but God is not impressed and "brings the princes to nothing" (Isaiah 40:23). "There are many devices in a man's heart," Proverbs tells us, "nevertheless the counsel of the Lord, that shall stand" (Proverbs 19:21, KJV).

The weather in Tampa and Charlotte were reminders that "Our God is in the heavens: he hath done whatsoever he hath pleased" (Psalm 115:3, KJV). When they come unexpectedly and when they scatter the powerful of the earth, storms underscore human limitations and divine omnipotence. They force us to consider the amazing transcendence of God and they are a sign of his impregnable will—even among the nations of the earth. They remind us that we are all weaklings in the hands of a mighty Maker.

In recounting the miracles of deliverance for Israel from Egypt, the psalmist writes: "The clouds poured down rain ... Your thunder roared from the whirlwind; the lightning lit up the world! The earth trembled and shook" (Psalm 77:17, 18, NLT).

Yes, we must be mindful of politics—and its importance in our lives. But we must always place our final trust not in politics but in Providence. When God spoke above Tampa and Charlotte, he wanted us to remember that.

September, 2012

*L*et This Be Our Prayer

It came during dark days. It came in the midst of war—war as we had never seen it, before or since.

It came to a nation bitterly divided.

The resolution had passed the United States Senate on the third of March. Now it was on the President's desk for his signature. It called for a Day of National Humiliation, Fasting, and Prayer.

The year was 1863. It was the third year of the Civil War.

President Abraham Lincoln had not grown up as a particularly devout man. In fact, early in his political career, he was forced to defend charges that he was an "open scoffer at Christianity." Although the deaths of two sons, one just the previous year, had deepened Lincoln's faith in "Divine Providence," it could hardly have been said that the president was an avid Christian, especially during the pious mid-nineteenth century. He had not, for example, joined any church, though he did occasionally attend a Presbyterian church in Washington.

Now, as the bloody conflict raged on, and three months after signing the Emancipation Proclamation that officially ended slavery, Lincoln prepared to issue another presidential proclamation. The words were eloquent. They were also stark. The president, who never wore his religion on his sleeve and never paraded it to garner votes, spoke truth to power. In his message, he revealed more spiritual insights and wisdom than many religious leaders—then or now.

Lincoln wrote that "nations, like individuals, are subjected to punishments and chastisements in this world." He argued that "the awful calamity of civil war, which now desolates the land, may be but a punishment inflicted upon us for our presumptuous sins."

Lincoln revisited the theme of God's judgment in his Second Inaugural Address. In this proclamation, he pointed out that America had been blessed with "the choicest bounties of Heaven" and "preserved these many years in peace and prosperity. We have grown in numbers, wealth, and power as no other nation has ever grown."

Then the president dropped the hammer.

"But we have forgotten God," Lincoln wrote. "We have forgotten the gracious hand which preserved us in peace, and multiplied and enriched and strengthened us."

One might be tempted to think that Lincoln was familiar with the warning of Moses to the people of Israel found in the book of Deuteronomy:

"For when you have become full and prosperous and have built fine homes to live in, and when your flocks and herds have become very large and your silver and gold have multiplied along with everything else, be careful! Do not become proud at that time and forget the LORD your God, who rescued you from slavery in the land of Egypt" (Deuteronomy 8:12-14, NLT).

Like Moses, Lincoln laid the responsibility for national seriousness and remembering in the hands of the citizens themselves. Like an Old Testament prophet, he rebuked a forgetfulness brought on by the arrogance of success.

"We have vainly imagined, in the deceitfulness of our hearts, that all these blessings were produced by some superior wisdom and virtue of our own," he said. "Intoxicated with unbroken success, we have become too self-sufficient to feel the necessity of redeeming and preserving grace, too proud to pray to the God that made us!"

If Lincoln wrote that in 1863, what would he say of us today?

The richest, greatest, and most powerful nation on earth has neglected and trivialized worship, boasted of its own ingenuity and achievements, secularized Sunday, and elevated and enriched those who are, to use Lincoln's own term, "open scoffers at Christianity." Our culture revels in debauchery and our national government continues to legislatively legitimize all manner of sexual immorality and—in the name of freedom—approves a virulent hostility toward religion.

Never in our history have we been more materially rich and spiritually destitute. It's been aptly observed:

> NEVER IN OUR HISTORY HAVE WE BEEN MORE MATERIALLY RICH AND SPIRITUALLY DESTITUTE.

"We worship our work, work at our play, and play at our worship."

Lincoln was a leader who understood and respected the power and holiness of a sovereign God who had his own way with nations—even one as great as the United States. He had suffered tragic personal loss and had seen bloodshed on a massive scale. He knew it was a fearful thing to fall into the hands of the living God.

Every year in May, America commemorates a National Day of Prayer. God tells us that national healing and spiritual renewal begin with "my people, who are called by my Name" (2 Chronicles 7:14). Christians should be the very first to heed Lincoln's call:

"It behooves us then, to humble ourselves before the offended Power, to confess our national sins, and to pray for clemency and forgiveness."

Let this be our prayer for America.

May, 2012

$\mathscr{W}$here Angels Fear to Tread

M y dad, who loved stories, always chuckled about the farmer whose
cow was hit by a passing motorist.

Apologetic, the driver asked if he had done any damage to the cow.

"Well," the farmer drawled, "if you did her any good, I'd be glad to pay
you for it."

That's sort of what happened when Pastor Robert Jeffress introduced Texas
Governor Rick Perry to a group of evangelical Christians in Washington DC.

Dr. Jeffress, the outspoken senior minister of First Baptist Church in Dallas, asked the Values Voter Summit:

"Do we want a candidate who is a good, moral person—or one who is a
born-again follower of the Lord Jesus Christ?"

To clear up any confusion or doubt, Pastor Jeffress declared that "for evangelical Christians, there really isn't any choice" other than Govenor Perry
(with apparently no due respect to Congresswoman and former presidential
candidate Michelle Bachmann, a devout born-again Christian). "Every true,
born-again follower of Christ ought to embrace a Christian over a non-Chris-
tian," Jeffress told the crowd.

Pastor Jeffress later told reporters that he believed Mormonism to be "a
cult" and that Mitt Romney, a Mormon, was not a Christian.

Rick Perry said of Jeffress' speech that the pastor had "knocked it out of the park." Then the governor immediately began distancing himself from Jeffress' foul ball. Govenor Perry "does not believe Mormonism is a cult," his campaign spokesman said.[11]

The damage control was under way and Pastor Jeffress was suddenly in the national news.

I greatly admire Robert Jeffress as a caring pastor, conservative theologian, and as an outstanding preacher. Beth and I often listen to him on the radio while on the way to our own church on Sundays. That's why I found his remarks—and his intemperate rush into presidential politics—surprising, disappointing, and inappropriate.

Anyone can make a mistake. That's what God's grace is all about. Pastor Jeffress made a mistake. Here's why:

1. It is unwise for any minister to endorse a candidate for public office. It is an abuse and a denigration of the pastoral role—both in the church and in the community. It is arrogant for a pastor to presume to use the pulpit to tell people who to vote for. It compromises the cause of Christ and the spiritual integrity of the church.

2. The U.S. Constitution expressly forbids the very qualification that Jeffress has publicly trumpeted. The authors of our founding document were clear and firm on this point:

"No religious test shall ever be required as a qualification to any office or public trust under the United States" (Article Six).

3. Although Pastor Jeffress has repeatedly asserted that most of our founders were evangelical Christians, and America was founded as a "Christian nation," a careful and balanced examination of the historical record points to quite the opposite.

Most of our founders were deists, meaning that they believed in God as a "Supreme Being," but not necessarily a personal one. Most of them viewed Jesus Christ as a great moral teacher and prophet but stopped short of personally embracing him as Lord and Savior. If Madison, Washington, Hamilton, Franklin, Adams, and Jefferson were alive today, it's not very likely that any of them would attend First Baptist Dallas—or any other evangelical church.

If Pastor Jeffress' presidential litmus test of being "a born-again follower of Christ" had been strictly applied to those who have occupied the White House, we probably would not have had Washington, Adams, Jefferson, Jackson, Lincoln, FDR, Eisenhower, or Kennedy.

As for one of our greatest presidents, Theodore Roosevelt was a firm believer in the separation of church and state and attempted to have "In God We Trust" removed from American coins because he considered it unconstitutional and sacrilegious.

If we applied Pastor Jeffress' test, there would be no Mount Rushmore.

If one reads history objectively, there is no other conclusion to reach than that America was founded as a godly and moral nation, but not as an expressly Christian one.

> AMERICA WAS FOUNDED AS A GODLY AND MORAL NATION, BUT NOT AS AN EXPRESSLY CHRISTIAN ONE.

4. The reason Rick Perry immediately distanced himself from Jeffress' remarks is because they damaged his campaign at a time when it had been damaged enough. Pastor Jeffress was trying to help Perry. Instead he had given the Texas governor one more controversy to explain away.

Ministers need to walk a very wide and prudent path around politics.

The apostle Paul warned Timothy about good soldiers not becoming "entangled in the enterprises of civilian life" (2 Timothy 2:4, Amplified Bible). They can be a divisive distraction.

Jesus told his followers to be "wise as serpents and harmless as doves" (Matthew 10:16). Unfortunately, Pastor Robert Jeffress, in this instance, was neither.

And if he did Rick Perry any good, I'm sure the governor would be glad to pay him for it.

October, 2011

ℐacred Fire

If things had gone differently, he could have been hanged as a traitor. As it turned out, he led a hopelessly outmatched army to improbable victory and the grateful people of a newly independent nation hailed him as their hero. When the fifty-five men who gathered in Philadelphia to create a new government needed a presiding officer, there was no other logical choice.

Two years later, after the framers of the American Republic wisely rejected the idea of six chief executives and settled on one, he was elected our nation's first president—by acclamation. He was so revered by his countrymen that his rise to leadership in the nation he cherished was uninterrupted and natural.

George Washington had plenty of ambition, but his dignity and integrity kept it well concealed.

On April 30, 1789, Washington stood on the balcony of Federal Hall in New York City and placed his right hand on an open Bible to take the presidential oath of office. The cannon and the wild cheers of the crowds embarrassed him and, following the ceremony, he quickly entered the hall to deliver his inaugural address to a joint session of the newly formed House and Senate. He was not an orator—without a prepared text he was at times inarticulate—and his gift was not brilliance as much as it was an incorruptible character.

He spoke simply, clearly, and from his heart about his journey to this time and place.

Washington told Congress that he had planned to remain retired at Mount Vernon, which he described as "the asylum of my declining years." Yet he had been "summoned by my country, whose voice I can never hear but with veneration and love…" He spoke with a candid humility about his "conflict of emotions"; being overwhelmed with "despondence… inheriting inferior endowments from nature and unpracticed in the duties of civil administration…"

Such professed inadequacy today wouldn't win you the Iowa straw poll.

Washington then told Congress that, in view of the "weighty and untried cares before me… it would be… improper to omit in this first official act my fervent supplications to that Almighty Being who rules over the universe, who presides in the councils of nations, and whose providential aids can supply every human defect…"

> **WASHINGTON REMEMBERED WHAT SOLOMON KNEW AND HAD PRAYED FOR: WISDOM TO LEAD.**

When God asked the new King Solomon what he wanted, Solomon told the Lord that "I am but a little child; I do not know how to go out or come in… So give your servant an understanding heart to judge your people, to discern between good and evil. For who is able to judge this great people of yours?"(1 Kings 3:7, 9, NASB).

Washington remembered what Solomon knew and had prayed for: wisdom to lead.

The first president also recognized that God had directed the creation of the new nation:

"No people can be bound to acknowledge and adore the Invisible Hand which conducts the affairs of men more than those of the United States." Washington conceded that "every step" along the path toward American independence had "been distinguished by some token of providential agency."

As today's culture wars in America are re-ignited over issues such as religious freedom, abortion, contraception and gay marriage, some—even respected conservatives—have argued that there is no place for a discussion of private morality in political discourse; that there is no appropriate public debate over the importance of cultural values in our society.

Washington would have disagreed.

In his first statement to the American people as their first leader, the new president spoke of his conviction concerning the essential interdependence of morality and success:

"There is no truth more thoroughly established than there exists in the economy and course of nature an indissoluble union between virtue and happiness; between duty and advantage..." Our first president told his countrymen that "the smiles of heaven can never be expected on a nation that disregards the eternal rules of order and right which heaven itself has ordained..."

It was an observation as relevant and as important as the next presidential debate or White House news conference.

And then the man, who had so conspicuously pledged his life, his fortune, and his sacred honor to the greatest experiment in self government in the history of the world, offered a challenge to us all:

"...the preservation of the sacred fire of liberty and the destiny of the republican model of government are... entrusted to the hands of the American people."

That's something to remember as we choose George Washington's next successor.

February, 2012

The Things That Matter Most

It was a cold and gray day.
It was also historic.

The American nation was struggling through the worst economic crisis of its history. Unemployment wasn't eight percent—it was twenty-five percent. Millions of people had given up hope. Families were desperate, children were hungry, farmers were broke. It was a national catastrophe. Some wondered openly if perhaps this was the end of the American experiment—the end of free men and free markets; the collapse of capitalism and our way of life.

Millions of others pinned their hopes on this one man—the new president.

On March 4, 1933, Franklin D. Roosevelt spoke to a country on the brink of ruin and gripped by fear. He electrified the nation with his confidence and, of course, he addressed the economic crisis at his inaugural on the steps of the U.S. Capitol.

But Roosevelt did more than that. He spoke of morality.

While he knew that the economy was people's chief concern, FDR also understood that his success in the crisis—and the success of his country—depended on something far greater than mere plans and policies. He needed to rally his fellow citizens around a shared vision–a moral one. As he looked out upon the crowd of sullen and anxious faces, Roosevelt said of the difficulties: "They concern, thank God, only material things."

The new president went on: "Happiness lies not in the mere possession of money; it lies in the joy of achievement, in the thrill of creative effort."

Roosevelt's appeal was nearly spiritual.

"These dark days," he said, "will be worth all they cost us if they teach us that our true destiny is not to be ministered unto but to minister to ourselves and to our fellow men." He reminded his troubled nation "that we cannot merely take but we must give as well…"

FDR appealed to "old and precious moral values" in inspiring the courage and determination required to face and surmount the crisis. That appeal to shared values would be successfully made once again when "the greatest generation" won victory for freedom in the most significant war in history.

Citing FDR's comment about "material things," Richard Nixon observed at the end of the tumultuous sixties:

"Our crisis today is the reverse. We have found ourselves rich in goods, but ragged in spirit."

There are those who will seek the nation's highest office today who believe that it is the spirit of America—not just her economy—that needs reviving.

> THE CHRISTIAN KNOWS BETTER THAN TO THINK THAT OUR NATION'S CURRENT CRISIS IS ONLY ECONOMIC. THE HISTORY OF CIVILIZATION, THE HUMAN CONDITION, AND THE BIBLE ITSELF TELL US DIFFERENTLY.

They have had the courage and the vision to challenge the orthodoxy that moral issues don't matter. They have honestly spoken about the destructive pathologies of divorce, welfare dependency, and single parenting that are tragically undermining the American family. They have defended religious freedom. They have also warned of the dangers posed to our children by such evils as pornography.

For displaying this unconventional courage, they have been assailed by those with big money and small ideas.

The Christian knows better than to think that our nation's current crisis is only economic. The history of civilization, the human condition, and the Bible itself tell us differently.

The Scriptures declare that "righteousness

exalts a nation: but sin is a reproach to any people" (Proverbs 14:34, NKJV). It may be ancient, but this is an admonition that even the greatest of nations ignore at their peril.

Jesus said: "Be careful and guard against all kinds of greed. Life is not measured by how much one owns" (Luke 12:15, NCV). Neither is national greatness. Without freedom, without faith, and without family, economic strength is not only meaningless—it is impossible.

Let us pray that the president of the United States will have the courage and integrity to tell us the truth about ourselves and the land we love—to remind us that by both freedom and responsibility a shared culture is built and that our greatness as a republic is anchored in national and personal morality.

Let us pray in this nation for a return to the things that matter most—those virtues that never change.

March, 2012

Chapter Four: That Special Time of Year

"The best and most beautiful things in the world cannot be seen or even touched. They must be felt with the heart."

HELEN KELLER

$\mathcal{M}$ile Markers

Portland: 40 miles.

Augusta: 30 miles.

Waterville: 15 miles.

As we passed each sign, I would turn to my weary wife and smile. "We're almost home, honey—just a few more miles!"

When I drove a lot more than I do now, I longed for those mile marker signs. They encouraged me. They told me how far I'd come and let me know how far I had to go to reach my destination. And when my destination was home, especially when I was traveling alone on a cold January night in Maine, I loved to see those numbers going down. They kept me awake. They kept me going. They marked my progress along I-95.

There are two important annual mile markers in our lives: the New Year and our birthdays. If any of us are ever tempted to get reflective about life—and contemplation is pretty rare these days—those might be the occasions. These are the times when we stop and look back. We see where we've been. We think about the critical choices we've made and how they've shaped our lives. Hopefully, we count our blessings.

When we turn the other way and peer into an unknown future, we compare how fast the past twenty years have sped by and we contemplate where we might be at the end of another twenty. And whether it's the beginning of a New Year or we're blowing out birthday candles, there is often the resolve to live better lives: to live more wisely, more productively, more charitably. We resolve to change, to become better men and women in the coming year.

As we get older—as the miles posted on the signs of our lives start going down—we think more about time and mortality. While God is not at all bothered or restricted by time, he understands our preoccupation with it. And he wants us to value it.

God is immortal and the Bible says he has placed eternity in our hearts. Still, we are very much bounded by mortality. Perhaps we should think more about eternity than we do. But we don't grasp it very well and so, instead of contemplating forever, we think about today—and all the things we've got to do. And we think about how we don't have much time, so we better hurry. Time flies—and so do we!

Solomon described the hectic and unreflective life: he called it "chasing the wind."

We would do well, as we race down life's highway, to ease up a bit on the accelerator and notice the mile marker signs. And to take some stock in our lives. We may be exceeding the speed limit.

Moses prayed in the ninetieth Psalm: "Teach us to realize the brevity of life…" The King James puts it like this: "Teach us to number our days."

Why?

"So that we may grow in wisdom" (Psalm 90:12, NLT). So that we might make right choices and set right priorities.

God has numbered our days—and he's set our appointment with eternity. He wants us to also number our days so that we might be wise in how we spend them.

> EACH NEW DAY IS A PRECIOUS GIFT AND AN INCREDIBLE BLESSING. EACH NEW DAY IS AN EXCITING OPPORTUNITY. LET'S LOOK AT OUR LIVES THIS WAY. THE WAY GOD LOOKS AT THEM.

The follower of Jesus Christ has the chance to live every single day for him—to think as he would think, to act as he would act, to serve as he would serve, and to love as he would love.

The Bible tells us over and over again that life is not just brief—it is terribly uncertain. We are warned against presumptuous living.

We may "grow in wisdom" when we remember that we've only got so many of these twenty-four-hour periods left to us. And we have no idea how many.

Each new day is a precious gift and an incredible blessing. Each new day is an exciting opportunity. Let's look at our lives this way. The way God looks at them.

Someday, we'll all reach home. Keep an eye on those mile markers. And enjoy the trip.

December, 2010

$\mathcal{M}$att Henry's Diary

I remember when it happened to Beth and me while we were attending a conference in Boston—a Christian conference, no less!

We were robbed!

Before we could get back to our van in the parking garage under our hotel to get the rest of our belongings, someone had poked out the door lock and reached in and taken Beth's winter coat and a sweater I had just bought the day before and had yet to wear. We were outraged; we had been violated!

Never mind the fact that it happens to millions of Americans every year, it had happened to *us*! And it had never happened to us before. We had carefully locked the van. We thought we were protected from theft, at least for about twenty minutes. We couldn't believe it.

I'm sure it was an equally unpleasant—and much more dangerous—experience when Matt Henry was robbed one night. He was held up at gunpoint. His wallet was stolen. We don't know if Mr. Henry went to the police. There's no record of it. What we do know is that Matt Henry went home later that evening and made an entry in his diary.

"Tonight, I was robbed and I am thankful," he wrote. "Let me be thankful, first, because I was never robbed before; second, because although he took my wallet, he did not take my life; third, because although he took all

I possessed, it was not much; and fourth, because it was I who was robbed, not I who robbed."

We know this because "Matt" Henry was Matthew Henry, the famed early eighteenth-century Bible expositor whose masterful commentaries on both the Old and New Testaments won the praise—and extensive use—of such giants as George Whitfield, Charles Wesley, and Charles Spurgeon. On the night he was robbed, Henry was riding on horseback—heading through the woods for a church service, where he was to be the guest preacher. His subsequent journal entry became famous as an example of "giving thanks in all things."

I was a bit curious about what was in Henry's commentary under 1 Thessalonians 5:18: "Be thankful in all circumstances, for this is God's will for you who belong to Christ Jesus" (NLT). While Rev. Henry died in 1714, before he could get this far in his epoch work, other writers gathered his extensive notes and completed the commentary. Here are the comments they gathered under this text:

"If we pray without ceasing, we shall not want matter for thanksgiving in everything. As we must in everything make our requests known to God by supplications, so we must not omit thanksgiving. We must be thankful in every condition, even in adversity as well as prosperity. It is never so bad with us but it could be worse. If we have ever so much occasion to make our humble complaints to God, we never can have any reason to complain of God, and have always much reason to praise and give thanks."

We don't write like this anymore. Sadly, not enough of us think and act like this either. The rampant virus of entitlement has infected our postmodern age, and it has even infiltrated the church, robbing us (you might say) of our gratitude.

> THE RAMPANT VIRUS OF ENTITLEMENT HAS INFECTED OUR POSTMODERN AGE, AND IT HAS EVEN INFILTRATED THE CHURCH, ROBBING US (YOU MIGHT SAY) OF OUR GRATITUDE.

How many of us truly believe, as Matthew Henry obviously did, that thankfulness is a duty before it is a feeling? Robert Louis Stevenson was right: "The man who forgets to be grateful has fallen asleep in life."

I could have used more of Matt Henry's attitude in Boston that day. It's not always easy, of course, but the Thanksgiving season might be a good time for all of us to ask God for help in being more thankful—in every situation.

Matt Henry's diary is a great example.

November, 2010

When Peace Comes

They are leaving.

Except for some support for our diplomatic corps, all remaining American troops in Iraq are coming home.

President Obama made that promise during his campaign and now he's honoring his pledge. For many families, this is glorious news—the return of their sons and daughters from a dangerous and distant land. For others, it will be a time to remember the loved and the lost. More than four thousand young Americans died in the ten-year war in Iraq. They died for their country. They died for freedom and for justice. Many others will bear the scars of war for a lifetime.

While we all hope and pray for peace and stability in Iraq, it may yet prove to be an elusive goal. From the League of Nations to the United Nations, and from the Alliance for Progress to nuclear disarmament, peace has been a far easier dream than it is an achievement.

In war, as in all else that falls short of the ideal, the heart of the world's problem is a problem of the heart. The prophet Jeremiah was blunt in his description of the fallen nature of man: "The heart is deceitful above all things, and desperately wicked; who can know it?" (Jeremiah 17:9, KJV).

Therein is the rub in politics and policy: despite his genius, man's soul is depraved. Humankind's best efforts to secure "peace on earth and goodwill toward men" fall short so often because we all fall short. Greed, pride, and the lust for power, control, and domination have always stoked the fires of military aggression. And there is no evidence to suggest that man will "evolve" to a point where the lamb will not need to fear the lion. We close another turbulent year of the twenty-first century with a multitude of fresh reminders that war and violence are still very much with us, both at home and abroad.

So where is the hope?

Seven hundred years before his birth in Bethlehem, Jesus Christ was named the "Prince of Peace." When the chorus of angels joined in exultation on that brilliant night of his birth, declaring "peace on earth," they were celebrating the coming of the ultimate peacemaker. The angels were confirming that lasting peace—between nations and between individuals—could only come (and that it would indeed someday come) when the peace of Christ entered into every human heart. This peace would not merely be the cessation of hostility, but the "Shalom of God," as the Jews call it.

Jesus Christ was born to bring peace to the soul. He came to put an end to striving and warring within. Jesus came so that you and I could have peace at the center of our lives, secured not through written treaties, but by faith in the one who commands the storms of life, "Peace, be still!"

This same Messiah will someday bring a permanent peace to this earth. Men will then study war no more. The lion will lie down with the lamb. As our efforts to find peace through diplomacy continue, as they should, our final faith is in the Christ who will one day reign as king. "Of the increase of his government and peace there will be no end" (Isaiah 9:6).

> AS WE CELEBRATE CHRISTMAS, MAY OUR FAITH AND HOPE REST SECURELY IN HIM WHOSE BIRTH WE HONOR—THE CHRIST WHO WILL TRIUMPH YET.

In the darkest days of the Civil War, the poet Longfellow wrote the song "I Heard the Bells on Christmas Day":

> *"And in despair I bowed my head: 'There is no peace on earth,' I said. 'For hate is strong, and mocks the song of peace on earth, good will to men.' Then pealed the bells more loud and deep: 'God is not*

dead: nor doth he sleep; the wrong shall fail, the right prevail, with peace on earth, goodwill to men.'"

As we celebrate Christmas, may our faith and hope rest securely in Him whose birth we honor—the Christ who will triumph yet.

Because we know that one day lasting peace will come. And His blessings will flow "as far the curse is found."

May you and your family enjoy a wonderful, Spirit-filled Christmas.

December, 2011

The Triumphant Truth of Christmas

We've had fair warning about Christmas.

Like the New Hampshire primary, the start date keeps getting moved back. I have seen Christmas displays in stores in August. Thanksgiving stands up against commercialism. After all, how do you market a holiday based on the idea that we should give thanks for what we already have?

Christmas? It's almost a pagan ritual. Two things have contributed to the increasing secularization of our most significant and sacred holiday. First, American multiculturalism and pluralism, combined with political correctness, have led to the idea that Christmas is alongside several other religious holidays that must be given equal billing. Christmas may be special to some, but it's not as special as it used to be. And it certainly is no longer exceptional. The public schools reflect this trend toward inclusive sensitivity, and the rest of society is slowly getting the message.

The other factor, of course, is money. The expansion of the season is not because we want more time to contemplate the meaning of Christmas, but because we want more time to buy and sell. This is the inevitable result of the postmodern marginalization of religion generally, and Christianity in particular. If spirituality matters less and is more relative in our lives, won't Christmas suffer as a result? It will and it has.

For Christians, the challenge is to appreciate Christmas more, not less. It is to seek, amidst the engulfing superficialities, a deeper understanding of the central spiritual truths that Christmas represents. When Charles Dickens closed his wonderful story by telling us that Scrooge resolved to keep Christmas in his heart, it reminds us that this is our chief duty. We must grasp the meaning of the incarnation, in our hearts and in our minds.

The wonder, the meaning, and the spirit of Christmas must never become casual in our lives. God became one of us and entered the world he created. This should always amaze us. Jesus told Philip, "Anyone who has seen me has seen the Father" (John 14:9).

This should always overwhelm us. That Jesus Christ is the Savior of the world should always lead us to praise God for his unspeakable gift. It matters not how trivial or shallow Christmas may become in the eyes of others. For the Christian, Christmas must always be a Very Big Deal, and a continual source of joy and exaltation. Christmas must live in our hearts every day of the year.

> GOD BECAME ONE OF US AND ENTERED THE WORLD HE CREATED. THIS SHOULD ALWAYS AMAZE US.

A teenager who a few hundred years ago told his father he thought the church needed better and more contemporary music, wrote a song that should never go out of fashion. Isaac Watts captured the joyous theology of the one event in history that proves the existence and the incredible love of God:

"Joy to the world! The Lord is come; let earth receive her King."

This is definitely not politically correct.

But Watts presses on nonetheless. He writes about how "the Savior reigns" and that Jesus Christ has come "to make his blessings flow far as the curse is found." This is no diminutive tribal god or prophet made out of man's vivid imagination. This is man's eternal salvation. This is the incomprehensible and comprehensive Creator of the universe. And Watts happily acknowledges him without fear of contradiction. His reign is global:

"He rules the world with truth and grace, and makes the nations prove the glories of his righteousness, and wonders of his love."

This is beauty. But it is more than beauty. It is truth. And it is triumphant truth.

This is why Christmas is the most wonderful time of the year. And it is the most wonderful news any time of the year.

December, 2011

When Gratitude Is Tested

Young Martin found his gift—and its expression—as a singer and composer at the well-known St. Thomas Church of Leipzig, Germany.

He worked his way through the University of Leipzig and, upon obtaining his degree, Martin Rinkart was ordained as a Lutheran minister at the age of thirty-one.

It was 1617 and the powerful winds of the Protestant Reformation were sweeping across Europe. For thirty years, wars and dissension would wrack the continent. From major cities to small villages, violence took a devastating toll.

Rinkart was assigned a pastorate in his hometown. Because it was a walled city, Eilenburg was seen as a safe haven for thousands of refugees fleeing the threat of war. Yet over time, the city lost its capacity to absorb the dramatic influx.

Instead of being a place of refuge, Eilenburg became a tragic cauldron of death and disease. Overcrowded and underfed, the city was unable to provide even the basic necessities of food, medical care, and adequate sanitation. Hundreds of people succumbed to the spreading pestilence.

Pastor Rinkart was a steady encouragement to his weary parishioners. He served and comforted them, with tender faithfulness, as a loving shepherd to a troubled flock. In the midst of their suffering, Rinkart composed more than sixty hymns of hope and faith. He entertained his church with plays centered on the Reformation. He led his congregation to see the transcending love and power of God, even in the tragic circumstances of their lives.

With fear and despair haunting every street corner of Eilenburg, Martin Rinkart was a pillar of courage, love, and persevering faith.

But his greatest test was yet to come.

In 1637, a dark plague settled across the city and threatened to wipe it out. When other ministers either died or fled, Rinkart was left alone. He buried more than four thousand men, women, and children that year, sometimes conducting as many as forty-five funerals in a single day. One was for his wife.

It was a daily horror that staggers the modern imagination.

But there is an amazing irony to the rest of this story that forever rescues it from meaningless tragedy and raises it to the heights of joyful triumph.

It was during this year that Martin Rinkart wrote his most famous hymn, probably composed between funerals. It's title? "Now Thank We All Our God:"

> *"Now thank we all our God, with heart and hands and voices, Who wondrous things hath done, in whom his world rejoices; Who from our mother's arms, hath blest us on our way, with countless gifts of love, and still is ours today."*[12]

"Now thank we..." Really?

"Who wondrous things hath done." Really?

"His world rejoices." Really?

"Countless gifts of love..." *Really?*

Such an attitude in these tragic circumstances is so far beyond the contemporary mind-set as to seem strangely out of touch. Thankfulness in the middle of this? What could poor Rinkart possibly have been thinking? This was hardly a life of unlimited possibilities.

Perhaps Martin Rinkart was thinking as a Christian should think, feeling as a Christian should feel, and believing as a Christian should believe.

PERHAPS MARTIN RINKART WAS THINKING AS A CHRISTIAN SHOULD THINK, FEELING AS A CHRISTIAN SHOULD FEEL, AND BELIEVING AS A CHRISTIAN SHOULD BELIEVE.

The apostle Paul tells us to "be thankful in all circumstances, for this is God's will for you who belong to Christ Jesus" (1 Thessalonians 5:17, NLT). It is the inclusive nature of this command that is its ultimate test.

Gratitude comes hardest in adversity.

It was in the midst of the worst of all human adversity that the pen of Martin Rinkart burst forth in glorious praise and gratitude for the goodness of God. And when thousands of people lift their voices to sing this beautiful hymn at Thanksgiving—in this country and around the world—they get a glimpse into the heart and mind of the man who passed, with flying colors, the greatest test of gratitude.

"O may this bounteous God through all our lives be near us; with ever joyful hearts and blessed peace to cheer us. And keep us in his grace and guide us when perplexed; and free us from all ills in this world and the next."

November, 2011

$\mathcal{W}$hen Streets Are Dark

D ecember 24, 1941 was not an easy Christmas Eve.
Three weeks earlier, the Japanese had attacked Pearl Harbor and
the United States had entered the Second World War. Americans were on
edge, facing an uncertain future that would call forth the greatest united sacrifice in the nation's history.

British Prime Minister Winston Churchill made a dangerous secret voyage to Washington D.C., to visit the man with whom he would forge a close
friendship through the fires of global conflict: Franklin Roosevelt. Under
clear and cold skies, the two world leaders appeared together on the balcony
of the White House. Twenty thousand had joined them for the lighting of
the Christmas tree.

No one had expected Churchill to be there. Because of the secrecy of his
trip, his name was left off the official program.

After President Roosevelt lit the tree, he spoke to the crowd:

"How can we light our trees? How can we give our gifts? How can we meet
and worship with love and with uplifted spirit and heart in a world at war, a
world of fighting and suffering and death?"

After telling his fellow Americans—including many listening by radio—
that he had declared January 1 as a Day of Prayer for the nation and the

world, the president answered:

"Our strongest weapon in this war is that conviction of the dignity and brotherhood of man which Christmas Day signifies—more than any other day or any other symbol."

Prime Minister Churchill then rose to speak:

"This is a strange Christmas Eve. Almost the whole world is locked in deadly struggle, and, with the most terrible weapons which science can devise, the nations advance upon each other... Here, in the midst of war, raging, and roaring over all lands and seas... here, amid all the tumult, we have tonight the peace of the spirit in each cottage home and in every generous heart. Therefore we may cast aside for this night at least the cares and dangers which beset us..."

On Christmas Day, the president and the prime minister went to church, where they sang "O Little Town of Bethlehem."

Churchill had never heard the song.

It was written by American clergyman Philips Brooks following his visit to Jerusalem in 1865. On Christmas Eve, Brooks went by horseback to a mountain where the shepherds were said to have kept their sheep. This visit was the inspiration for his famous carol. Describing the silent beauty of the small village where Jesus was born, Brooks then wrote these words:

"Yet in thy dark streets shineth the everlasting Light—The hopes and fears of all the years are met in thee tonight."

Hopes and fears have often struggled against each other.

The two men who would lead the world in reclaiming freedom knew that for all the fears engulfing the globe on that Christmas Eve of 1941, hope was an even greater force—because of what had happened in Bethlehem nearly two thousand years before.

God had entered the world. The angel proclaimed to terrified shepherds the Good News of great joy. And this Good News

> CHRISTMAS SYMBOLIZES THE TRIUMPH OF COURAGE OVER FEAR, OF HOPE OVER DESPAIR, AND OF LOVE OVER HATE.

would be for all people everywhere. Christ the Savior had been born! Christmas symbolizes the triumph of courage over fear, of hope over despair, and of love over hate.

The streets of our world—and of our lives—are sometimes dark. Yet in those streets and at those times, the everlasting light of Jesus Christ shines. The apostle John tells us that no matter how powerful the darkness may often seem, it can never extinguish the light of Christ. "There is no fear in love," John tells us. "But perfect love casts out fear" (1 John 4:18).

And nowhere was God's perfect love more fully, more beautifully, or more powerfully displayed than in that "Little Town of Bethlehem" on the night when Christ was born.

December, 2010

Acknowledgment goes to distinguished historian David McCullough and his excellent book In the Dark Streets Shineth.

*O*ne Unwavering Resolution

Not long ago, I was looking through some old family photo albums. What memories! And what a reminder that everything changes. It's the one constant in life.

Our days—and the lives of those around us—are a fast-flowing current. They never stay the same.

We embark upon a new year with high hopes. I've heard more than one person say, "I hope it's a better year than this last one!" Admittedly, that's a negative way of putting it, but the hope is still there.

One thing's for certain: the next year will be different. Sure, there will be routines, but something will be different. We will be different. The world will be different.

Change will come every day.

Speaking before the State Agricultural Society in Milwaukee, Wisconsin in 1859, Abraham Lincoln told this story:

"It is said an Eastern monarch once charged his wise men to invent him a sentence, to be ever in view, and which should be true and appropriate in all times and situations. They presented him the words: 'And this, too, shall pass away.' How much it expresses! How chastening in the hour of pride! How consoling in the depths of affliction!"

Nothing—and no one—remains the same.

What will this mean for us personally? What will it mean spiritually? What should it mean?

"Be at war with your vices," wrote Benjamin Franklin, "at peace with your neighbors, and let every new year find you a better man."

The apostle Paul speaks of this constructive character advancement in the opening passage of his letter to the Philippians:

"And I am certain that God, who began the good work within you, will continue his work until it is finally finished on the day when Christ Jesus returns" (Philippians 1:6, NLT).

God leaves none of us unfinished. He continues his work.

God wants to guide the change within each of us. He wants this year to end with our individual improvement. He wants to make us "better men"—and women.

How can we be partners in God's personal transformation of our lives?

Paul writes to the Philippians:

"I pray that your love will overflow more and more, and that you will keep on growing in knowledge and understanding. For I want you to understand what really matters, so that you may live pure and blameless lives until the day of Christ's return" (Philippians 1:9,10, NLT).

"I pray that... you will keep on growing... For I want you to understand what really matters..."

> PAUL BECKONS US TO THE OPEN WATERS—OUT BEYOND THE SAFE HARBORS—UPON THE HIGH SEAS OF SPIRITUAL ADVENTURE AND GROWTH.

Love, growth, understanding, a sense of priorities. This is what Paul wishes for the Philippians. It's what Paul hoped and prayed for in the life of every Christian believer: spiritual maturity.

How? For the great apostle, it all came down to one unwavering resolution:

"I want to know Christ and experience the mighty power that raised him from the dead" (Philippians 3:10, NLT).

To know Christ is to grow and mature as a believer. To know Christ is to show love and grace. To know Christ is to have the right priorities in our lives. To know Christ is to know how to live as his disciples.

There is much in this world—and, tragically, in the Church—to keep us existing in shallow harbors. Paul beckons us to the open waters—out beyond the safe harbors—upon the high seas of spiritual adventure and growth.

In order that we may become better men and better women.

We can't hope to change the world until we are changed.

For the Christian, to change is to be more like him. May this be our unwavering resolution for the coming year.

January, 2010

$\mathscr{W}$hen the Stone Moved

It was big—so big it had to be rolled into place on a track.

It was hard, heavy, impenetrable, immovable, and cold. In its silent intimidation, the stone that was rolled in front of Jesus' tomb seemed to symbolize the triumph of death and decay.

The stone was intended to seal the grave of Jesus. It represented a final verdict: dead and gone.

At the Pharisees' request, amid speculation that his followers would attempt to steal Jesus' body and falsely claim his resurrection, Pilate posted Roman soldiers to guard the tomb. It was as if Satan himself was protecting his prey.

But the stone was rolled away. Very early in the morning, before the sun rose, the stone began to move.

And then *the Son* rose!

Why does this matter? What difference does it make that the stone moved? What difference does it make that the tomb is empty—still empty after more than two thousand years?

The empty tomb makes all the difference in the world—and all the difference in our lives.

When the stone moved that first Easter morning, it spelled the difference

EVERYTHING ELSE | 125

between fear and courage; between futility and meaning; between despair and hope; between death and life.

In the language of sports and politics, the resurrection of Jesus Christ is the ultimate "game-changer."

Satan and his team had done all within their power to win. They rubbed their demonic hands with delight and danced around the fires of hell as the Son of Man was arrested, put through the mockery of a "trial," tortured beyond human imagination and endurance, and then hung upon a cross to die.

> THAT WOULD HAVE APPEARED TO BE IT— THE END. BUT THE DEVIL HAD UNCORKED THE CHAMPAGNE A BIT TOO EARLY.

That would have appeared to be it—the end. But the devil had uncorked the champagne a bit too early.

Just as the evil one was raising his glass in diabolical celebration, suddenly in the misty stillness of a cemetery the stone began to move. While I love all the gospel accounts of the greatest event in human history, I appreciate Matthew's unique description of that morning.

Only he tells us that things didn't remain peaceful for long:

"And behold, a severe earthquake had occurred, for an angel of the Lord descended from heaven and came and rolled away the stone and sat upon it. And his appearance was like lightning, and his clothing as white as snow. The guards shook for fear of him and became like dead men" (Matthew 28:2-4, NASB).

Matthew says that the earth shook. Indeed, in many more ways than simply geological.

I especially like Matthew's depiction of how the angel descended from heaven "and came and rolled away the stone..."

Get this: "...and sat on it." I picture the angel crossing his legs and arms in smiling defiance.

And what of the world's most powerful empire?

"The guards shook for fear of him and became like dead men."

Jesus had made a clean sweep of death, destruction and the devil—and all earthly powers!

Game over.

Paul told the Corinthians that God had masterminded the resurrection triumph "for our ultimate glory before the world began" and that if "the rulers of this world" had "understood it…they would not have crucified the Lord of glory" (1 Corinthians 2:7-8).

But they didn't understand. God took them by surprise.

When the stone moved, it confirmed the truth about Jesus Christ. He predicted his own death and resurrection. The resurrection proves Jesus is who he claimed to be.

When the stone moved, it confirmed the truth about our salvation. The first disciples of Jesus believed he had risen—and they claimed to have seen him in bodily form. They preached his resurrection, they taught it, and they gave their lives for its truth and declared that Jesus was the only savior of the world.

And when the stone moved, it also confirmed the truth about our hope—today and forever. In the Old Testament, centuries and centuries before Jesus, Job asked, "If a man die, shall he live again? If so, this would give me hope through all my years of struggle…" (Job 14:14, NLT). The empty tomb answered Job's question—and ours. We don't need to fear death. Jesus has defanged it.

Yes, what a difference that morning made—that morning when the stone moved.

April, 2012

Chapter Five: No Greater Love

*"There is no greater love than to lay down
one's life for one's friends."*

JOHN 15:13, NLT

*"The only people who will be really happy are those who
have sought and found how to serve."*

ALBERT SCHWEITZER

$\mathscr{G}$entlemen

They were Christians. They were thinkers. They were leaders. They were humble giants.

They were my heroes.

Former United States Senator Mark Hatfield and English pastor John Stott passed away within two weeks of each other in 2011. Hatfield was eighty-nine. Stott was ninety.

Mark Hatfield served as Republican Governor of Oregon in the early 1960s before representing that state in the U.S. Senate for thirty years. The son of devout Baptists, Hatfield's experience as a Navy officer during World War II made a powerful and unforgettable impact on him. After commanding amphibious landings on Iwo Jima and Okinawa, Hatfield was among the first to witness the city of Hiroshima after the dropping of the atomic bomb.

The "utter devastation in every direction," as he later described it, was seared into Hatfield's memory and led him to become an uncompromising adversary of war and violence. In the Senate, Hatfield's principled opposition to the Vietnam War made him a national figure.

John Stott served quietly and faithfully as the rector of All Soul's Church in London for more than fifty years. It was his only pastorate. Yet his incisive and thoughtful preaching and writing attracted an international following.

Stott didn't seek fame, lived simply, and never let his reputation go to his head. He spent three months of every year for half a century writing in a remote cottage in Wales. The result was fifty books that helped to shape evangelical Christianity for the second half of the twentieth century.

Following the publication of Stott's 1958 classic, *Basic Christianity*, Queen Elizabeth appointed him a chaplain to the throne. Still, Pastor Stott remained a humble and self-effacing churchman. "An evangelical is a plain, ordinary Christian," he said. And that is how he lived—privately and publicly.

As a preacher and pastor, Stott held consistently to a high view of the authority and life-changing power of the Bible as God's inspired, revealed Word. "Every authentic ministry begins... with the conviction that we have been called to handle God's Word as its guardians and heralds," he wrote. "Our task is to keep it, study it, expound it, apply it, and obey it."[13]

When I was contemplating a career in elective public service during college, Mark Hatfield's book *Conflict and Conscience* persuaded me that a Christian could be in politics without compromising his faith or losing his soul. "My faith," Hatfield wrote, "is both an inward journey to find the true purpose of my own life and an outward journey to be of service to others."[14]

That was my journey too. Mark Hatfield, by his words and his Christian example, influenced me to enter political life.

When I first became a pastor, John Stott's book *Between Two Worlds* helped me to understand the vital importance of preaching in the life of the church. He wrote: "I believe that nothing is better calculated to restore health and vitality to the Church or to its members into maturity in Christ than a recovery of true, biblical, contemporary preaching... Preaching is indispensable to Christianity."[15]

It led to my lifelong love affair with the spoken Word.

In the summer of 2008, when God called me to start Grace Heritage Community Church, I spent several hours one night in the parking lot of a hamburger joint reading Stott's final book—a recollection of his pastoral ministry entitled *The Living Church*. It was Stott in his eighties—and at his best:

"There is such a thing as goodness: pursue it. The postmodern world is unfriendly to all universal absolutes. Yet the apostle says there is such a thing as truth: fight for it. And there is such a thing as life: lay hold of it. May God enable us to make an unabashed commitment... to what is true, what is good and what is real."[16]

Mark Hatfield, politician and statesman. John Stott, pastor and preacher. They were men of courage and integrity; they were scholarly and dignified men of compassion and humility. They thoughtfully and faithfully lived out their Christian faith. They could disagree with others and remain civil. They were men of substance. They made large marks upon their times. I admired them, studied them, and was inspired by their words and deeds. Like King David, these Christian leaders lived to "a good old age, full of days... and honor" (1 Chronicles 29:28).

> THEY WERE MEN OF COURAGE AND INTEGRITY; THEY WERE SCHOLARLY AND DIGNIFIED MEN OF COMPASSION AND HUMILITY.

Both of these great men of faith lived by an ancient creed that seems tragically missing in so much of today's divisive turmoil:

"The Lord has told you what is good, and this is what he requires of you: to do what is right, to love mercy, and to walk humbly with your God" (Micah 6:8, NLT).

They were class acts. They were true gentlemen.

August, 2011

$\mathscr{F}$orrest Knew

There's that scene in the movie. You remember it.

Forrest Gump has welcomed his girlfriend, Jenny, to the lovely family homestead in Greensboro, Alabama. Childhood friends, they are grown now and Jenny's come in from a very cold and stormy life to the warm haven of an innocent friendship she knew many years before.

Forrest, who has carried a torch for Jenny with simple nobility and a fierce loyalty that is clearly unrequited, now professes openly his love to her. He asks her to marry him. She sadly deflects his affection, knowing things about herself that she cannot share. Forrest is adamant. He tells her:

"I may not be a smart man, Jenny, but I know what love is."

It was just one of the many profound and touching moments in a film that won Tom Hanks an Oscar.

Do we "know what love is?"

It's a good question in a culture that is losing its struggle with superficiality. Forrest Gump was possessed of a love that was deep, pure, and unadulterated. His heart had always drawn a straight line through all of his extraordinary experiences. And that line led him to Jenny.

Love has too often fallen prey to the fallacies and excesses of the age. It's always been a mystery, of course, even in simpler times. But today, it's harder than ever to get a grasp on first things. The combination of advancing technology and falling mores has left life's greatest virtue in a state of eclipsed uncertainty.

Instead of trying to rediscover the true meaning of love, we sometimes are tempted to ask, like the song, "What's Love Got to Do With It?"

But God hardly regards love as a "second-hand emotion."

> ## GOD HARDLY REGARDS LOVE AS A "SECOND-HAND EMOTION."

The apostle John writes that "love comes from God. Anyone who loves is a child of God and knows God." John's whole first letter is an ode of tender beauty to the primacy of love. He goes so far as to assert that "anyone who does not know love does not know God..." (1 John 4:7-8, NLT).

That's quite a pre-condition.

Valentine's Day is the florist's and confectioner's favorite day of the year. For Christians, it would be a good time to reflect on the greatness and glory of love. We should take it as an occasion to remind ourselves that God's whole relationship with humankind is based on love.

His love.

"This is real love," John tells us, "not that we loved God, but that he loved us and sent his Son as a sacrifice to take away our sins" (1 John 4:10, NLT). Our capacity to "know what love is"—the ability to love our spouse and our children and others—is rooted in the love of God that finds its fullest proof in the cross and its greatest expression in our hearts.

Why does John insist that only those who love can truly know God? Because, the apostle says, "God is love." It's a simple but deep truth that Forrest Gump would appreciate.

February, 2010

The Last Full Measure

The nightmares went on occasionally his whole life.

In the middle of the night, he would wake up screaming, yelling, and sometimes swearing.

My dad was back on Iwo.

At seventeen, he had lied about his age so he could join the Marines. Two years later, in February, 1945, he found himself in the midst of some of the fiercest fighting of the Second World War: the Battle of Iwo Jima. Some of my earliest memories are the stories Dad told me about being there. While he was also on Saipan and Tinian, he spoke more about Iwo. He told me about what it was like, about the friends he lost, and the close calls he had.

"War stories."

We are tempted to lightly dismiss them. For those who lived through them, they could never be dismissed—or forgotten.

When the film *Saving Private Ryan* came out, I went to see it. While it is a masterful, inspiring movie, I decided I'd never want my dad to see it, and he never did. A friend recently told me that when his father-in-law, who had been part of the Normandy invasion, saw the film and was asked if it was realistic, he said: "The only thing missing was the smell. You never forgot the smell."

There are fewer and fewer veterans from World War II still living. My dad left us three years ago. "The Greatest Generation" is fading away. But they are not the only heroes. I have two brothers-in-law who served in Vietnam. My son-in-law is a Marine who has been in both Iraq and Afghanistan.

Each year when we mark Memorial Day, brave men and women are still standing and fighting for freedom. Let's remember them. Let's thank them. Let's pray for them.

"I will teach you hidden lessons from our past," writes the psalmist, "stories we have heard and known... we will not hide these truths from our children; we will tell the next generation..."(Psalm 78:4, NLT).

John Adams said he hoped future generations would never forget the great price that was paid to secure their freedom.

JOHN ADAMS SAID HE HOPED FUTURE GENERATIONS WOULD NEVER FORGET THE GREAT PRICE THAT WAS PAID TO SECURE THEIR FREEDOM.

We all see plenty of flags around Memorial Day. When I stand for our national anthem and place my hand over my heart and look at our flag, I often think about a skinny and scared nineteen-year-old kid from Maine, trying desperately to stay alive on the black sands of an island he had never heard about. And I wonder what raced through his mind when he looked up and saw those same stars and stripes waving bravely at the top of Mount Suribachi.

Our sixteenth president was invited to share "a few appropriate remarks" at the dedication of a cemetery for the war dead at Gettysburg. He didn't speak long, but he sure made it count. We were in the midst of our bloodiest and most tragic war. Young men on both sides—all of them Americans—were fighting for a cause they believed in, for a way of life. Some weren't sure why they were fighting.

Lincoln was sure.

In his closing words, he told us what we must always remember. And he told us why:

"It is rather for us to be here dedicated to the great task remaining before us—that from these honored dead we take increased devotion to that cause for which they gave the last full measure of devotion—that we here highly resolve that these dead shall not have died in vain—that this nation, under

God, shall have a new birth of freedom—and that government of the people, by the people, for the people, shall not perish from the earth."

Take time to remember. And thank God for all those who have served.

May, 2010

Classic Jesus

"He wrote in the dust with his finger."
That was it.

They kept demanding that he declare himself. That he take sides. But he remained silent. When he finally did speak, it wasn't what they expected at all. It wasn't an "either or," "black and white" response.

The apostle John tells us in the eighth chapter of his gospel that the Pharisees interrupted Jesus as he was teaching the crowd. They dragged before him a young woman who had been caught in the act of adultery. They were trying to trap him into saying something they could use against him. "'Teacher,' they said to Jesus, 'this woman was caught in the act of adultery'" (John 8: 3-6, NLT).

Then came the trap:

"'The law of Moses says to stone her. What do you say?'" (vs. 5).

Our words can trap us sometimes. So can our thinking. We get boxed in by our prejudices, our pride, and our stubbornness. We narrow our choices and our options. Whether in our homes, our politics, or our churches, we too often throw up walls rather than try and build bridges. Jesus wrote in the dust with his finger. But he seldom drew a line in the sand, especially when someone was trying to box him in.

Jesus enjoyed getting outside the box. He encourages his followers to do the same.

When the Pharisees asked him who would be married to whom in heaven, Jesus pointed out that there would be no marriage in heaven. When they asked him about paying taxes, he was neither a Tea Partyer nor a big spender: he showed them a coin and said simply: "Give to Caesar what belongs to Caesar, and give to God what belongs to God" (Matthew 22:21, NLT). He left it to us to figure out which was which.

Was Jesus simply a muddled compromiser unwilling to take a stand? Certainly not: he was dogmatic and bold about many things. Jesus was crystal clear, for example, about the need for repentance, the sin of self-righteousness, and the one way to heaven.

While Jesus took strong positions on many things, he always thought before he spoke. He was deliberate. Jesus also offered unexpected and creative responses. He rejected simplistic answers and always made people think about their own position—and their own lives. He challenged snap judgments. He went beneath the surface of things.

Jesus encouraged introspection and self-examination. While there are some things that are black and white, Jesus appreciated the reality that his disciples live in a world with plenty of subtle gray.

Jesus was always compassionate. He was always loving. He was always forgiving. It may seem strange to say this about God incarnate, but Jesus modeled maturity in his dealings with people.

> JESUS ENCOURAGED INTROSPECTION AND SELF-EXAMINATION. WHILE THERE ARE SOME THINGS THAT ARE BLACK AND WHITE, JESUS APPRECIATED THE REALITY THAT HIS DISCIPLES LIVE IN A WORLD WITH PLENTY OF SUBTLE GRAY.

The apostle Peter tells us: "He is your example, and you must follow in his steps" (1 Peter 2:21, NLT).

And what about the young woman, the bait in the Pharisees' trap? If Jesus said, "Stone her!" he would conform to the law but show that he was unloving. If Jesus said, "Let her go!" he would show his compassion but disrespect the law.

A lose-lose proposition. But Jesus had another idea.

"All right," he calmly told them, "but let the one who has never sinned throw the first stone" (John 8:7, NLT). It was a third way—creative, unexpected, and profoundly wise.

It was classic Jesus.

April, 2010

$\mathscr{G}$ood Medicine

You wouldn't think it would make a difference.

Lilly Gillon was a British two-year-old suffering from a rare form of cancer. When she received life-saving medical help at a hospital in Oklahoma City, Lilly's parents were impressed with the warm hospitality of the people in the Sooner state. Lilly's spirits seemed good. When she returned to England, however, she didn't appear quite so happy.

Then back in Oklahoma for a vacation with his little girl, Lilly's dad noticed a marked improvement in her responsiveness. The more the folksy Oklahomans made over her, the more cheerful Lilly became. "They were just so nice," Graham Gillon remarked. In fact, the people in Oklahoma were so nice—so kind and friendly toward the whole Gillon family—that the Gillons began seriously considering moving there in order to speed Lilly's recovery.

Is there a connection between kindness and healing?

The Bible tells us that "a cheerful heart is good medicine, but a broken spirit saps a person's strength" (Proverbs 17:22, NLT). What about somebody else's cheerfulness? What about another person's strength? Can our kindness make a difference? Does it impact others? Perhaps more than we might think.

We influence people's dispositions—their attitudes, their spirits, even their health—in so many subtle ways. A warm smile, a firm handshake, or a hug or a tender word of thanks or encouragement can make all the difference in how somebody else gets through her day. A simple and sincere compliment can offer hope in ways you may never realize.

WE INFLUENCE PEOPLE'S DISPOSITIONS—THEIR ATTITUDES, THEIR SPIRITS, EVEN THEIR HEALTH—IN SO MANY SUBTLE WAYS.

We seldom know what's inside another person's heart or mind. The burdens people carry—their worries and concerns, their loneliness or heartache—are often known but to them and to God. This is especially true of the many strangers we briefly encounter along life's busy pathway.

There's simply a whole lot of hurt in this world that you and I don't know about. But broken spirits are mended by cheerful hearts. When we dispense kindness—especially to a stranger—we share some good medicine.

God instructed the Israelites to show kindness to foreigners: "But the stranger who lives among you shall be unto you as one born among you, and you shall love him as yourself." God then reminded his people that "you were strangers in the land of Egypt" (Leviticus 19:34, NKJV). When someone's far from home and all that is familiar, the kindness of a stranger means a lot. The writer of Hebrews tells us: "Don't forget to show hospitality to strangers, for some who have done this have entertained angels without realizing it" (Hebrews 13:2, NLT).

Francis Bacon wrote: "If a man be gracious and courteous to strangers, it shows he is a citizen of the world, and that his heart is no island cut off from other lands, but a continent that joins them."[17]

It costs us little to be kind—it is an inexpensive medicine. "If you give even a cup of cold water to one of the least of my followers," Jesus said, "you will surely be rewarded" (Matthew 10:42, NLT).

Of course, reward was not on the minds of the friendly people in Oklahoma when they reached out to precious Lilly Gillon and "loved on her." Their motive was not to gain but to give. Lilly and her family will not remember many of the folks who showed their kindness to them while they were strangers in a foreign land. Their paths may never again cross this side of eternity. But every word of cheer and encouragement, every smile and every act of kindness was noticed—and it was recorded. Perhaps the people of Oklahoma entertained an angel without realizing it.

Carry kindness with you every day. As God opens an opportunity, show some to others. It may not seem like much but it may make someone else feel a whole lot better.

Kindness is good medicine.

March, 2012

Off the Field

It is said that bad news gets around the world twice before good news gets its shoes on in the morning.

In our technologically advanced and morally challenged age, who would disagree with that? Bad news is omnipresent. We are saturated with tales of vice and violence, of corruption and compromise and cruelty. We must flee the TV and Internet if we are to hang onto any semblance of hope.

There is one bit of good news, however, that is everywhere prevailing against the tide of our dismay. Like a tender plant sprouting through the hardened soil of our cynicism, a young athlete has captured the world's imagination. Tim Tebow, former Heisman Trophy winner, NFL quarterback, and devoted Christian, has reached beyond football into our popular culture.

"Tebow Time"–the now-famous, down-on-one-knee-with-head-bowed prayer stance—has been mimicked around the globe. This earnest and gifted young gentleman has inspired millions of evangelical Christians.

He's also received some stinging criticisms from those who are less than impressed by his pious displays.

Tebow is a good quarterback who has achieved some stunning, usually last-minute, feats on the field. These have helped to gain him increased attention. But it is his activities off the field—his genuine kindness and generosity toward others—that has won the grudging admiration (and sometimes withering scorn) of the watching world. He has reached out to children and adults who are sick, injured, or disabled. By simply being a good and decent man who really cares, Tim Tebow has made a difference in their lives and in the lives of their families.

We've been reminded that when it comes to Christian faith, authenticity is both a test and a reward. While Tebow seems, to the most skeptical, too good to be true, he does appear to be what he claims to be: a deeply committed follower of Jesus Christ who consistently lives out his faith—on and off the football field.

> WE'VE BEEN REMINDED THAT WHEN IT COMES TO CHRISTIAN FAITH, AUTHENTICITY IS BOTH A TEST AND A REWARD.

Given the controversies in the world of professional sports and the soiled reputations of past heroes, Tebow's uncompromised virtue is newsworthy. Good news? Yes. And Tebow not only believes in the Good News and shares the Good News, he lives it. Even the harshest critics have yet to uncover any sham or hypocrisy in his personal life.

Tim Tebow is a genuine inspiration.

Veteran sportswriter Rick Reilly admits:

"There's not an ounce of artifice or phoniness or Hollywood in this kid Tebow, and I've looked everywhere for it... I've given up giving up on him. I'm a 100 percent believer. Not in his arm. Not in his skills. I believe in his heart... "[18]

"Let your good deeds shine out for all to see," Jesus said in his Sermon on the Mount, "so that everyone will praise your heavenly Father" (Matthew 5:16, NLT).

As for the critics who mock Tebow's goodness, the apostle Peter gave sound advice for us all:

"For so is the will of God, that with well-doing you may put to silence the ignorance of foolish men" (1 Peter 2:15, KJV].

There are many other fine Christian athletes who live out their faith. And it would be a mistake to think that Tebow's performance as a quarterback is somehow premised on his Christianity.

God doesn't measure us by yardage gained or lost, or by points scored.

In Tim Tebow's life—and in our own—it's not the dazzle of the field that matters most to God. It's the daily reality of a life lived well off the field.

God says through the prophet Jeremiah:

> *"Don't let the wise boast in their wisdom,*
> *or the powerful boast in their power,*
> *or the rich boast in their riches.*
> *But those who wish to boast*
> *should boast in this alone:*
> *that they truly know me and understand that I am the Lord*
> *who demonstrates unfailing love*
> *and who brings justice and righteousness to the earth,*
> *and that I delight in these things"* (Jeremiah 9:23,24, NLT).

Wherever his life and gifts may lead Tim Tebow in the years to come, let's pray that they always lead him to the cross.

January, 2012

$\mathcal{G}$od's Amazing Grace

It was a cold and rainy New England day in early spring 1996. The wind was whipping across the airfield.

I peered out at the small plane bouncing toward a landing. It taxied to the entrance of the airport in New Haven, Connecticut. That's when I first saw him. He was wearing a tan raincoat and carrying a briefcase. He was accompanied by a young aide.

Charles W. Colson, whose professed dramatic conversion to Christianity I had questioned as a college student years before, was coming to speak at Yale Law School. As the newly appointed Connecticut and Rhode Island director for Colson's Prison Fellowship Ministries, I was there to greet him and escort him to the event. Since my days in politics, I knew you greeted a VIP with a firm but deferential handshake. So I extended my hand to the smiling and energetic guest.

I instantly found myself enveloped in a bear hug. "Brother Jack," Colson enthused, "so great to meet you!" I was a bit startled. No formality—just authentic warmth. But when you've gone from being the Special Counsel to the President of the United States to wearing a prison uniform, you don't stand on a lot of formality.

When Colson was introduced to the packed law school auditorium, the students thought it would be clever to show a clip from the film *All the President's Men*, about the Watergate political scandal. In the scene played that afternoon, Robert Redford, who plays *Washington Post* reporter Bob Woodward, was quizzing a senior editor, played by Jack Warden.

"Who is Charles Colson?" Redford asked. Warden responded: "The most powerful man in the United States is President Nixon. You've heard of him?" Redford nodded. "Charles Colson is special counsel to the President. There's a cartoon on his wall. The caption reads, 'When you've got 'em by the [expletive], their hearts and minds will follow.'"

The students laughed and Colson smiled. When he took the podium, he was gracious and humble. "I appreciate that unique introduction," he said. "But I want you all to know that was the pre-Christian Colson, not the post-Christian Colson." The students laughed again.

It was a great beginning to Colson's thoughtful and polished exposition of Christianity and the transformative difference Christ makes in the life that surrenders to him. Chuck then proceeded to answer the students' questions on a wide range of ethical and theological issues. As always, he left winning the respect of his audience—a respect earned time and again in a secular forum by this extraordinary man's keen intellect, courage, passion, and integrity.

When, in April 2012, Chuck Colson went home to be with the Lord and Savior he loved and served so well, at the age of eighty, most of the media recalled his "pre-Christian" activities as Richard Nixon's ruthless political operative, his conviction in the Watergate scandal, and subsequent imprisonment.

The church of Jesus Christ—in America and around the world—remembered and celebrated something far different. Chuck Colson emerged from the dark days of his humiliation with a deep and genuine faith in Christ that inspired Christians, won the grudging respect of nonbelievers, and ultimately helped to change the face of American politics—this time in a completely different and more positive way.

He promised those he served prison time with for seven months that he would not forget them. God used Chuck to make good on that promise through Prison Fellowship Ministries, which Colson founded in 1976. PF is reaching prisoners and their families with the Gospel in all fifty states and 113 countries. Chuck himself visited six hundred prisons in the United States and forty countries. And, until illness, he was in a prison every Easter.

Later, through his syndicated radio broadcast, *Breakpoint*, thirty best-selling books, and The Colson Center for Christian Worldview, Chuck became one of the most admired advocates of integrating biblical faith into all of life—including the raging debates over the critical social justice issues of our time. There has been no more effective champion of the Christian worldview.

CHUCK OFTEN SAID THAT "AMAZING GRACE" WAS "THE PRISONER'S NATIONAL ANTHEM." HE KNEW. HIS OWN INCREDIBLE LIFE WAS A MOVING TESTIMONY TO REDEMPTION'S AMAZING POWER IN CHRIST.

Chuck Colson was a man of humility and compassion—raised up by God from the pit of his own pride and despair to become one of the truly great leaders of the Christian church. His eloquent voice of reason and courage will be sorely missed.

Chuck often said that "Amazing Grace" was "the prisoner's national anthem." He knew. His own incredible life was a moving testimony to redemption's amazing power in Christ.

"I thank Christ Jesus our Lord," wrote another convert named Paul, "who gave me strength, because he trusted me and gave me this work of serving him. In the past I spoke against Christ and persecuted him and did all kinds of things to hurt him. But God showed me mercy, because I did not know what I was doing. I did not believe.

"But the grace of our Lord was fully given to me, and with that grace came the faith and love that are in Christ Jesus" (1 Timothy 1:12-14, New Century Version).

Perhaps the apostle Paul and Chuck Colson are at this moment rejoicing together with the angels in heaven for that divine grace that alone is able to save to the uttermost.

April, 2012

Chapter Six: Pressing On

"Forgetting the past and looking forward to what lies ahead, I press on to reach the end of the race and receive the heavenly prize..."
PHILIPPIANS 3:13,14, NLT

"We conquer not in any brilliant fashion;
we conquer by continuing."
GEORGE MATHESON

Joel, Peter, and Real Hope

You've got to admire Joel Osteen.

I was in bed the other night watching TV and flipping the channels. I counted Joel Osteen on three channels. And one of his venues was Yankee Stadium. Wow! There he was, each time smiling, poised, confident, elegantly dressed, speaking without notes. His message was the same. In fact, his message is always the same. It's always uplifting, simple, filled with joy. Osteen preaches hope and the Power of Positive Thinking.

Osteen is not the first preacher to hit a responsive chord—and become a national celebrity—preaching the Gospel of Hope. Norman Vincent Peale did the same thing from his influential pulpit in New York City a couple of generations ago. Robert Schuller has been similarly successful in more recent years.

So Osteen's message is not unprecedented. But then again, neither is any Gospel-based sermon. And while American statesman Adlai Stevenson once famously remarked, "I find Paul appealing but Peale appalling," it's clear that the message of hope always hits the heart, lifts the spirit, and calms the soul. And in these tough times, it's no wonder Osteen is packing his church and filling Yankee Stadium. People want—they need—to find hope.

The apostle Peter wrote about how God "has given us new birth into a living hope" (1 Peter 1:3, NIV). It's a very positive message. Peter talks about our "inheritance" in heaven that "can never perish, spoil, or fade" (1:4). But while he's writing about this hope, he also says that you and I may have "to suffer grief in all kinds of trials," and that these trials come into our lives so that our faith "may be proved genuine" (1:6,7).

Christian hope always leads to a positive attitude in any circumstance, even in the midst of difficulties. We will have problems and trials and heart-aches. The Bible teaches this. As excited as he was about our eternal hope, Peter himself went through a major crisis of faith in which he denied even knowing Christ. He ended his life as a martyr. Hope is not the absence of trials.

The true source of the power of positive thinking is not a hope that allows us to escape problems, but a hope that takes us through them. And while hope should result in positive thinking, positive thinking can never manufacture true hope or ever take the place of it.

> THE TRUE SOURCE OF THE POWER OF POSITIVE THINKING IS NOT A HOPE THAT ALLOWS US TO ESCAPE PROBLEMS, BUT A HOPE THAT TAKES US THROUGH THEM.

Biblical hope is not a psychological fabrication that we work ourselves up to. It is a spiritual reality rooted in the theological truth about our sinful condition, our repentance, and God's forgiveness. This is real hope in a real God in real life in a real world.

Sin and repentance need to be a central part to any biblical message about hope. Without the acknowledgment of our utter hopelessness, there can be no true hope in Christ. We must always remember that hope doesn't prevent difficulties and disappointments, but prevails in the midst of them. This is our victory. This is our true hope in Jesus Christ. And it will last forever.

"My hope is built on nothing less than Jesus' blood and righteousness; I dare not trust the sweetest frame, but wholly lean on Jesus' name. On Christ the solid Rock I stand; all other ground is sinking sand, all other ground is sinking sand."[19]

Now that's positive thinking!

April, 2009

In Due Season

In October 2010, Texas officially went from being a football state to being a baseball state.

For a time, at least.

When Colby Lewis pitched a final out to New York Yankees batter Alex Rodriguez—in a remarkable display of poetic justice—the Texas Rangers made history. It was an improbable journey for the baseball franchise. After fifty long and dry years, the Rangers were going to the World Series for the first time. It was a story full of grace and mercy, as well as perseverance and confidence.

The team credited manager Ron Washington for its historic achievement. Not too long before the victory over the Yankees, Washington nearly lost his job because of a one-night stand with cocaine. He happened to get picked for a random drug test and told Rangers President (and Hall of Fame pitcher) Nolan Ryan and General Manager Jon Daniels what he'd done. There were plenty of calls for Washington's firing, but Ryan and Daniels decided to give him a second chance. Washington united and inspired his team and led them to glory.

Rangers slugger Josh Hamilton, a recovered drug addict and born-again Christian, said of Washington: "He's not an addict. He just made a mistake."

Underdogs always thrill us. Perhaps it's the irony of the triumph and the fun of the unexpected that capture our imagination. We love rooting for them. Whether it's the smiling President holding the headline "Dewey Defeats Truman," a long-shot horse named Seabiscuit, or Rocky Balboa going the distance with the champ, we are inspired.

It's not just the improbability of the outcome. It's the heroic stamina, steadfastness, and perseverance of the contender that wins our hearts. The Rangers went season after season after season with "better luck next year." Ron Washington nearly lost it all. So did Josh Hamilton. But like the courageous American founders whose names they bear, these men didn't quit—even in the face of the longest of personal and professional odds.

> IT'S NOT JUST THE IMPROBABILITY OF THE OUTCOME. IT'S THE HEROIC STAMINA, STEADFASTNESS, AND PERSEVERANCE OF THE CONTENDER THAT WINS OUR HEARTS.

They showed courage and faith in the midst of adversity.

And so they are an example to us all of what it means to simply keep on keeping on.

"Don't be weary in doing what is right and good," Paul told the Galatians. "Because at just the right time—in due season—you will reap a rich harvest of blessing—if you don't give up" (Galatians 6:9). Paul told the Corinthians to "remain steadfast and unmovable" in doing God's work. Because, wrote Paul, God's work—no matter how great the obstacles or difficulties in performing it—is never in vain (1 Corinthians 15:58).

There had to have been many times over the preceding half century—probably at the end of another losing season—when those coaches and players wondered if they'd ever get their chance to win the whole thing.

But their time finally came. This was their winning season—all the sweeter and more thrilling for having been not easily or quickly earned.

Perhaps you've wondered if you'd ever get to the other side of your struggles, if your hard work and faithfulness would ever pay off. Don't give up. Trust God. Keep serving, keep believing, keep hoping.

Your winning season might be just around the corner.

October, 2010

The Strong Swimmer

A ndrew Wilson didn't give up.
Mighty good thing he didn't.

If he had, he would have died.

The twenty-five-year-old Australian fisherman was out in his boat when an unusually large wave swept him into the waters of the Pacific off the coast of New South Wales.

His boat just kept right on motoring into the distance. Wilson wasn't wearing a life jacket. He was five miles from shore.

With "adrenaline and just sheer determination," he managed to stay alive in shark-infested waters. Had it not been for that, the strong current would have taken him out to sea. He was finally rescued and had suffered only minor injuries. One of the local rescuers observed that "miracles do happen. Lucky he was a strong swimmer."

And what did Andrew Wilson say?

"I wasn't going to stop, so I just kept going."

Are you a strong swimmer?

If you were swept off your boat tomorrow into rough seas, far from shore, without a life jacket, would you "just keep going?" Or would you just give up? If your private world was shattered by tragedy and loss, would you become bitter and blame God, or would your faith in God and his promises—and your confidence in the love of Jesus Christ—keep you going?

Tough questions. We don't often think about them because all of us hope and pray that nothing bad will ever happen to us. We are tempted to embrace a "feel-good God" who is obliged to keep us from all harm or difficulty.

But is this true?

> GOD DOESN'T PROMISE TO KEEP US FROM DEEP WATERS. HE PROMISES TO KEEP US FROM DROWNING.

God doesn't promise to keep us from deep waters. He promises to keep us from drowning. God doesn't promise to keep us from going through fires of oppression. He promises to keep us from being burned up (Isaiah 43: 1-4).

Jesus was quite direct: "Here on earth you will have many trials and sorrows." Jesus spoke plainly to his followers about the reality of the fallen human condition. But he doesn't leave us without hope or comfort or protection. With the key biblical injunction "but," Jesus gives us a reason to smile in the midst of our sorrows:

"But take heart, because I have overcome the world" (John 16:33, NLT).

Yes, God will keep us. Our part is to "keep going." Because God will never do for us what he has given us the strength to do for ourselves. The Perseverance of the Saints is not just theoretical doctrine. It's also practical living. And nobody in the Bible talked more about perseverance than the apostle Paul.

Paul was a strong swimmer.

He told the Philippians that he hadn't arrived yet spiritually. He was still a work in progress, but progress was always his aim: "I focus on this one thing: Forgetting the past and looking forward to what lies ahead, I press on to reach the end of the race and receive the heavenly prize for which God, through Christ Jesus, is calling us" (Philippians 3: 13,14, NLT).

"I press on."

When he neared the end of his race, and his life—after swimming in many shark-infested waters and battling the rough currents of persecution, deprivation, and pain—Paul could write from his prison cell: "I have fought the good fight, I have finished the race, I have kept the faith" (2 Timothy 4:7). Paul didn't give up. Like Andrew Wilson, sometimes through his "adrenaline and just sheer determination," the great apostle "just kept going."

So the next time you ask God to keep you in your boat, safe and sound, remember one more prayer:

"Dear Lord, make me a strong swimmer."

March, 2011

$\mathcal{P}$opping the Clutch

I was ten years old, a gangly, skinny, and awkward kid who was tall for my age. I couldn't play sports, but I could reach the pedals.

I had been pestering my dad about wanting to learn to drive. So one day, following an afternoon of rabbit hunting with the two beagles, Dad said to me, "Jack, why don't you drive us home?" I was surprised but delighted. "Really?" I asked.

"Sure," he told me, "you've been wanting to learn how to drive, haven't you?"

I turned the key of his '50 gray Chevy fastback and felt the engine come to life. It may have been just a slant six, but it felt plenty powerful to me. I carefully put a foot on the brake and the clutch and slid the car into reverse. Then I placed my right foot on the accelerator and gently pressed down. I removed my left foot off the clutch—nervously, quickly.

The car stalled.

"Jack, let the clutch out slowly or you'll pop it and stall the car." My dad's voice was calm, with just a very minor note of agitation. "Now, let's do it again."

Again, I "popped the clutch" and stalled the old Chevy. My dad's voice was a bit more impatient but still determined. After repeating this practice four or five more times, with my dad's impatience rising with each failure to launch, I began to cry and told him I didn't need to drive.

"Jack, you can do this and you will," he said. "We're going to sit here all night until you drive this car. I know you can do it. Focus, listen carefully, and try again."

Finally, as I learned how to let the clutch out ever so gently and press on the accelerator just right, the car began to move. I got excited. The clutch was fully released. I pressed on the gas and edged out toward the road. I looked both ways (we lived in a rural area of Connecticut) and out I went. I shifted through the three gears without incident and drove the three miles home.

When I parked the car in our driveway and got out, I looked at my dad. He was grinning broadly. "Jack, I knew you could do it. Congratulations, son! See, it wasn't so bad. Aren't you glad you didn't quit? Now you know how to drive."

Well, not exactly. There were plenty more times over the next couple of years when my dad would watch with amusement as I bounced and lurched the car (or his Ford pickup) down some dirt road while we were out hunting. But in time I improved and passed my driver's test at sixteen the first time I took it—on a standard transmission.

I'm glad my dad didn't give up on me when I popped that clutch—even when I kept doing it. While I'm sure he wasn't pleased with my failures, he forgave me and insisted on giving me another chance. He told me he didn't want me quitting but to keep trying. And he stayed right there beside me, guiding me, encouraging me, and almost demanding that I start over each time the Chevy stalled. After repeated attempts, I learned how to drive that car, at least well enough to get it home. As my confidence and experience grew, I became a better driver.

Our heavenly Father watches us pop our clutch. He sees us stall out spiritually. But he never gives up on us. His grace, his love, and his patience give us another chance to get it right. He tells us that he loves us and that with his help and guidance—and through his strength—we can do it.

> GOD'S NOT DONE WITH US YET. HE WON'T QUIT ON US. AND HE DOESN'T WANT US QUITTING EITHER. HE KNOWS WE CAN DO IT.

Paul's encouragement to the Philippians are words that you and I must remember and live by:

"And I am sure that God who began the good work in you will keep right on helping you grow in his grace until his task within you is finally finished on that day when Jesus Christ returns" (Philippians 1:6, The Living Bible).

God's not done with us yet. He won't quit on us. And he doesn't want us quitting either. He knows we can do it.

Even when we pop the clutch.

November, 2010

Southpaw

Nobody expected it. Nobody thought it was realistic. Nobody would have predicted it.

It was quite a night for such a young man.

It was quite a night for baseball.

Derek Holland started pitching for the Texas Rangers in game four of the 2011 World Series. When he left the field eight and one-third innings later, the St. Louis Cardinals hadn't scored a single run. After losing the previous night by an embarrassing 16-7, the Rangers had come back strong, winning 4-0.

The series was now tied—thanks to a kid from York, Ohio who just turned twenty-five a couple of weeks before.

It was the stuff of dreams. And Derek Holland, though he hadn't had much of a career up to that point, had always dreamed of pitching in the World Series. In game four, his dream became a glorious reality and a lifelong memory—for Derek and for Ranger fans.

What made this Cinderella story even more amazing is the fact that Derek Holland is left-handed. Most pitchers—most people—are right-handed. Left-handers are in the minority. They're special, different, and unusual. But there Derek Holland was, under the pressure of the World Series and in the wake of an ignominious defeat, pitching up a storm—with his left hand—and leading his team to victory.

The next day, every left-handed kid in America was taking justifiable pride in being different. Derek Holland was different. And Derek Holland, at least for a day, was a genuine hero.

The Bible tells us of many people who were different—special in their backgrounds, their opportunities, their challenges, and their gifts. God repeatedly points to examples of underrated people and unexpected achievements.

Tucked away in the Old Testament book of Judges, we read of one such example. He even had a funny name—Ehud (pronounced "EEE-hud").

Like the Texas Rangers, the Israelites were in desperate need of a champion to deliver them. Because of Israel's sin—which unfortunately occurred at regular intervals, much like our own—God had given the nation over to its enemy. King Eglon of Moab kept Israel under his dominance for eighteen years. He imposed a severe tax on the Israelites.

We read in Judges 3:15 that "when the people of Israel cried out to the Lord for help, the Lord again raised up a rescuer to save them. His name was Ehud son of Gera, a left-handed man of the tribe of Benjamin" (NLT).

"A left-handed man."

It's fascinating that the scriptures would draw attention to this unusual physical distinction. In fact, the tribe of Benjamin had seven hundred left-handed men who made up the elite troops. Judges 20:15 tells us that "each of them could sling a rock and hit a target within a hairsbreadth without missing." (NLT).

Wow. I wonder if any of these guys was named Derek?

They sure didn't let being left-handed stand in the way of their prowess and accuracy.

The third chapter of Judges records how Ehud bravely killed the wicked king Eglon with a handcrafted, two-edged dagger—wielded with his left hand, of course. He also took command of an army of Israelites to challenge their oppressors. "Follow me," Ehud shouted, "for the Lord has given you victory over Moab your enemy" (Judge 3:28, NLT). And so he did.

Through a left-handed leader, God delivered a nation.

It was another example of interesting and unlikely heroes we discover throughout the Bible. Moses was wandering in exile in the desert, Gideon was hiding in the bottom of a winepress, David was a kid out in a lonely field tending sheep.

What is the source of this surprising and ironic heroism?

The apostle Paul talks about it in his first letter to the Corinthians:

> "Remember, dear brothers and sisters, that few of you were wise in the world's eyes or powerful or wealthy when God called you. Instead, God chose things the world considers foolish... God chose things... counted as nothing at all, and used them to bring to nothing what the world considers important" (1 Corinthians 1: 26-28, NLT).

NO MATTER WHO YOU ARE, NO MATTER WHERE YOU ARE, AND NO MATTER WHAT YOU ARE, GOD HAS A SPECIAL PURPOSE FOR YOU

Why does God choose in this way? Why does he revel in the unlikely?

"As a result, no one can ever boast in the presence of the Lord"(vs.29, NLT).

No matter who you are, no matter where you are, and no matter what you are, God has a special purpose for you and he wants to use you in some unexpected and extraordinary ways.

Just ask a southpaw named Derek Holland.

October, 2011

*I*mpossible

H e looked at me with surprise.
  "The State House of Representatives," I told him quietly.
"You're going to run against Roosevelt T. Susi?" he asked in disbelief.
"Yes, I suppose so," I replied.

When I had first asked for the nominating petitions, the town clerk assumed I was running for the local town council or perhaps the school board.

I was fresh out of college, a skinny, bespectacled kid who decided he wanted to get involved in politics. My opponent would be the former Majority Leader of the Maine House, former chairman of the powerful Taxation Committee and a fourteen-year legislative veteran. And his name was Roosevelt, no less! "Rosie" they called him. He was a distinguished and highly respected silver-haired statesman. I was a geek living with my parents. He was fifty-seven, I was twenty-three.

It was an impossible matchup.

I look back on that time with some wonderment. What was I thinking? Nearly everyone else was asking the same question. People found it amusing, my mother worried about the pain of losing, and nearly everyone figured it would be a good experience for a young man. Even the leaders of my own party laughed out loud—to my face.

But I took the risk.

I knew the outcome was in God's hands, so I wasn't afraid to step out and attempt the impossible. I had fun and knocked on every door in the three-town district over six months of daily campaigning. On Election Day, I won sixty-five percent of the vote.

I had tried the impossible and the impossible had happened.

They were right—it was a great experience for a young man. And it's a great experience for all of us—at any age. The missionary Hudson Taylor called it "attempting great things for God—and expecting great things from God."

When God tapped the frightened Gideon to deliver Israel from the Midianites, God wanted the victory to be his. "You have too many warriors with you," God told Gideon. "If I let all of you fight the Midianites, the Israelites will boast to me that they saved themselves by their own strength" (Judges 7:2, NLT).

God decided that the odds weren't impossible enough. So he winnowed out the troops. Gideon's army went from thirty-two thousand down to ten thousand. If a church dropped that much in Sunday attendance, it would be in a serious crisis. God's reaction to this dramatic reduction?

"There are still too many!"

So the army was cut again. This time, the numbers went from ten thousand to a mere three hundred. That was less than one percent of what Gideon had started with. The other 99 percent went home.

> ALWAYS REMEMBER THAT NOTHING GREAT WAS EVER ACHIEVED WITHOUT RISK, SOMETIMES CONSIDERABLE RISK—AND A WHOLE LOT OF FAITH.

God decided he liked those odds.

Of course, God gave victory to the Israelites—and he got the glory.

When the great British statesman Richard Cobden was told that repealing the country's oppressive corn laws would be impossible, he thundered to Parliament: "Impossible? If that is the only objection, I say let us move ahead!"[20]

There is a tendency as we grow older to be more cautious in risk-taking. Fear taunts us. We calculate the odds more carefully. Certainly, prudence has its place. But we must also always remember that nothing great was ever achieved without risk—sometimes considerable risk—and a whole lot of faith.

"You don't have enough faith," Jesus told his disciples. If they did, then "Nothing would be impossible" (Matthew 17:20, NLT). They once asked him who could possibly be saved. Jesus told them, "The things that are impossible with men are possible with God" (Luke 18:27, KJV).

When Abraham was told that Sarah would bear him a son even though she was ninety, she laughed on the other side of the tent. But the Lord was serious. "Why did Sarah laugh?" God asked Abraham. "Is anything too hard for the Lord?" (Genesis 18:13,14, NLT).

Well, is it?

There are some things God can't do. He cannot lie. He cannot fail. For all the rest there is but one response: "Lord, I believe; help thou mine unbelief" (Mark 9:24, KJV).

This week, this month, this year, why not step out and test your faith? Take it out for a drive. You may discover it is stronger and more powerful than you ever imagined.

Impossible?

"With God, nothing shall be impossible"(Luke 1:37, NLT).

February, 2011

*L*arry's Dream

L arry Hasenfus had a dream.

He always wanted to play college sports. Baseball was his favorite. But it never happened.

When Larry suddenly found himself out of work at the age of fifty-eight, he decided to go back to school and enrolled at Springfield College in Massachusetts. And then Larry did something really crazy. He decided to try out for the junior varsity baseball team. He had kept himself in good shape by playing hockey. Now he was going to reach for his long-deferred dream.

And good for him that he tried, because Larry made the team. Although he hadn't played baseball since high school, Larry's knuckleball earned him a place on the pitcher's mound. Larry beamed. His teammates were younger than his own kids, but Larry had no trouble keeping up. "It was always a dream for me to play college sports," he said.

"It was always a dream..."

What's yours?

The Bible describes it as "hope deferred" (Proverbs 13:12a). We call it a dream. And "a dream fulfilled is a tree of life" (vs. 12b).

Sometimes our dreams are fulfilled, sometimes not. One thing is certain: God loves us and he has a plan for our lives. That's become a sort of Christian cliché, but it's a fundamental truth of our life in Christ that in the midst of our disappointments we often forget. "Take delight in the Lord," the psalmist tells us, "and he will give you your heart's desires" (Psalm 37:4, NLT). That doesn't mean God will necessarily give us everything we want. It means he will give us everything we should want.

If our desires—our dreams—are in accordance with God's purpose for us, he will grant them—often against all human odds. Believing this is called trust.

God doesn't always work overnight, although he can and has. Usually God works over time.

Patience and perseverance are not virtues easily come by, especially today. But if you think of Grandma Moses (who became a

> GOD DOESN'T ALWAYS WORK OVERNIGHT, ALTHOUGH HE CAN AND HAS. USUALLY GOD WORKS OVER TIME.

well-known artist in her eighties), Colonel Sanders (who started a fried chicken business with his first social security check at sixty-five), J.C. Penney (who was advised to declare bankruptcy at age sixty-nine) and Winston Churchill (who was a political has-been in his sixties, just before he became British prime minister), then you remember that, in the end, life can be pretty special. "So the Lord blessed Job in the second half of his life," his biography tells us, "even more than in the beginning" (Job 42:12, NLT).

God frequently defers our hopes—and our dreams. But his timing, like everything else about him, is perfect.

God told the prophet Habakkuk:

"This vision is for a future time. It describes the end, and it will be fulfilled. If it seems slow in coming, wait patiently, for it will surely take place" (Habakkuk 2:3, NLT).

That's good advice—for prophets, who are not remembered for their patience, and for guys playing college baseball at fifty-eight.

Larry Hasenfus will tell you: dreams really can come true.

June, 2010

$\mathscr{F}$it for a King

The King's Speech is one of the very best films in recent years. It is well-directed, brilliantly acted, and it tells a compelling story in a compelling way.

When King George VI ascended the British throne at the end of 1936, on his brother's abdication, he was a very reluctant monarch. His severe, lifelong stuttering problem had undermined his self-confidence. The movie tells the fascinating account of how a little-known speech therapist helped the king overcome his impediment, gain his confidence, find his voice, and lead England to victory in World War II.

The film garnered twelve Oscar nominations, more than any other movie in 2010. Hollywood, which often produces imbecilic trash, gave due artistic recognition to filmmaking at its very best. A British film, perhaps, but still honored.

There are many things that draw you to the movie. It is set in historically decisive times for the whole world. The king's fear of public speaking is contrasted with the daunting challenge facing the British Empire. Hitler's mesmerizing platform presence dwarfs George's painful attempts at simple articulation. The stakes are high and the situation seems hopeless. The Nazi war machine rumbles across Europe and England's king can barely utter a single sentence of rally cry! It is a frustrating, sad, and yet moving spectacle.

Against all odds, the speech therapist, with a confidence bordering on joy, undertakes to improve the king's speech. It's not done overnight, but over time, after much strenuous practice and disciplined commitment, on the part of both the therapist and the king. The rest, as they say, is history.

George VI is not the only fearful person who has ever committed to undertake the near impossible.

When we face difficulties in our lives, it is necessary that we depend upon God as our source of strength and courage. Through his powerful Holy Spirit within us, we can meet any hardship and tackle any challenge. But we must also realize that it is equally imperative to do our part. We must pray as if the challenge ahead all depends on God. We must work as if it all depends on us. The therapist couldn't possibly have helped the king unless the king first wanted to help himself.

This is the most profound of New Testament teachings. We are told to stand, to resist, to fight, to carry on, to act, and to go forward. Sometimes we mistakenly think that God does it all and we do nothing. In the spiritual warfare to which we are called as soldiers, Paul tells us to "be strong in the Lord and in his mighty power" (Ephesians 6:10, NLT).

In this exciting and rewarding adventure we call the Christian life, we must never give up. Instead, we must press on. There were plenty of times that King George may have felt like giving up, that the obstacles of his personal impairment were too great to overcome. But this outstanding film draws its most moving inspiration from the perseverance of one man's private struggle to be victorious in his own life. The king had to claim this personal victory before he could lead his nation to victory.

> CROWNS ARE NOT JUST FOR BRAVE KINGS WHO OVERCOME. JESUS HAS ONE WAITING FOR EACH OF US WHO KEEPS ON KEEPING ON.

So too, you and I are called by Jesus Christ to overcome. We are called to persevere. We are called to continue. We are called to remain faithful, and never to give up—on God, his Word, or his love.

The same great apostle who told the Corinthians to "remain steadfast and unmovable" wrote from a prison in Rome as he neared death for the cause of Christ:

"I have fought the good fight, I have finished the race, and I have remained faithful. And now the prize awaits me—the crown of righteousness... which the Lord will give me..." (2 Timothy 4:7, 8, NLT).

Crowns are not just for brave kings who overcome. Jesus has one waiting for each of us who keeps on keeping on.

Never give up! Your reward will be fit for a king.

February, 2011

The God Who Is There

Opening Day.

It was an annual ritual. My Dad was a serious fisherman and he made detailed preparations that would rival Ike's at Normandy. I did not share my father's level of enthusiasm for fishing, although I sure do miss those times now. I suspect I'd appreciate being out all day in a boat on a beautiful lake a lot more than I did when I was ten.

By the time Dad and my brother and I drove to Maspaug Lake in Massachusetts from our home in northeast Connecticut, launched the boat, fully outfitted, and had lunches packed and life preservers at the ready, it was still pitch black—and chilly and damp. Dad wanted everything, right down to the flies tied at the end of the poles, all set for when the sun rose. As soon as it started getting light, we'd hear the command: "OK boys, let out your lines!"

We'd start to troll slowly around the lake. As the sun rose and the darkness receded, the fog also lifted. Things began to come alive. The sky turned blue, the air warmed, and there was a gentle breeze. Everything changed. And I would just look around in awe and admiration at all the beauty that God had made.

Those memories of Opening Day will stay with me forever.

When Jacob had his dream at Bethel in the twenty-eighth chapter of Genesis, he saw the stairway to heaven and heard the promise of God. God promised Jacob land and descendants. "All peoples on earth will be blessed through you and your offspring," God told Jacob. "I am with you and will watch over you wherever you go, and will bring you back to this land. I will not leave you until I have done what I have promised you" (Genesis 28:15, NIV).

When Jacob awoke, he was amazed. Then he spoke one of my favorite sentences in the whole Bible: "Surely the Lord is in this place, and I was not aware of it."

Sometimes our experiences are like mine on Opening Day. We are surrounded by dampness and darkness. We can't see the future. We may be fearful and uncertain. But then, in his perfect timing, God slowly lifts the darkness. We see the vistas of his beauty, the blue sky, and the warm sun. God melts the dampness and chases away the fog. He makes his way and his plan for us clear. He takes us through our trials, safely and gloriously to the other side. He gives us hope, encouragement, and renewed purpose. He reassures us of his everlasting love. He strengthens our faith.

> GOD MELTS THE DAMPNESS AND CHASES AWAY THE FOG. HE GIVES US HOPE, ENCOURAGEMENT, AND RENEWED PURPOSE. HE REASSURES US OF HIS EVERLASTING LOVE. HE STRENGTHENS OUR FAITH.

It's then we realize, just like Jacob, that God was there all along. "Surely, the Lord is in this place." Yes, in the place of our perplexity, God is there. In the place of our discouragement, God is there. In the place of our sadness and despair and our pain, God is there too. Like Jacob at Bethel, or like a ten-year-old in the darkness of Opening Day, it might not seem at first that God is in our place of need.

But always remember, he is the God who is there. In fact, he was there all along.

March, 2009

*R*un!

Wesley Korir knew what he was up against. And he knew what he had to do in order to make it.

"I had to hydrate to survive," Korir said. "I was more concerned about my hydration than my positioning."

The young Kenyan was the first of twenty-two thousand runners to cross the finish line in the 116th Boston Marathon. He ran it in two hours, twelve minutes, and forty seconds. It was the unusual heat (around 85 degrees) that kept Korir from beating the previous year's time of just over two hours. "It's hot out there, in case you didn't know it," he remarked with a broad smile after winning.

It was the heat Korir had to beat, and so he understood that what was in him was more important than what was ahead of him. Remaining hydrated was the key to his endurance. To finish strong meant he had to take care of himself along the way. He needed nourishment to keep his strength. Positioning would change throughout the race. Hydration was vital; dryness would be fatal.

Endurance is not easy. Sprints call for bursts of sudden energy and momentary enthusiasm. Sprinters are fast and the race is over soon. Marathons call for a different kind of strength. They require a resilience of spirit and a concentration of will. They require the iron determination not to give up—not to quit. Sprinters are in for a quick victory—marathoners for the long haul. It's a different mentality and a different expectation.

The reason the Bible has so much to say about the virtues of steadfastness, endurance, and perseverance is that the Christian life is not a sprint—it is a marathon. It is a journey, not a stroll; a voyage, not a ride around the lake. Truly following Jesus Christ is not an afternoon excursion, it's a lifelong expedition.

These are the metaphors of our faith—and for good reason. They describe the experience.

"The Christian life has not been tried and found wanting," observed G.K. Chesterton. "It has been found difficult and left untried." And so it is that many a professing believer starts out with the joyful enthusiasm of any fresh discovery. But in time zeal fades, commitment melts, and the joyful heart can languish. Even for those whose strength is renewed through the spiritual hydration of prayer and worship and the study of God's Word, there are still mountains to scale, valleys to enter, and deserts to cross. And who among us hasn't had to climb our own version of the Boston Marathon's Heartbreak Hill?

> GOD GIVES US HIS STRENGTH TO EMPOWER US AND HIS PRESENCE TO GUIDE US. HE HAS GIVEN US HIS SON TO INSPIRE US AND HIS HOLY SPIRIT TO RENEW US. GOD IS ALSO WITH US. GOD WILL HYDRATE US.

God would tell us that nothing great is ever easy. And he would be right.

But God would also be a cruel and detached stoic if he left it there. Because he loves us, God cheers us on. He encourages us not to give up. But God does more than this—so much more.

God gives us his strength to empower us and his presence to guide us. He has given us his Son to inspire us and his Holy Spirit to renew us. Every promise in the Bible is real and we may stand upon them, claim them, and live by them. God is not only for us—though it is great that he is.

God is also *with* us. God will hydrate us.

When the prophet Hosea calls for the people of Israel to repent and return to God, he offers the promise of renewal:

"In just a short time he will restore us, so that we may live in his presence."
Then Hosea says this:

"Oh, that we might know the Lord! *Let us press on to know him.* He will respond to us as surely as the arrival of dawn or the coming of rains in early spring" (Hosea 6:1-3, NLT, emphasis added).

"Let us *press on* to know him."

"We count them happy which endure," James writes (James 5:11, KJV). Scottish preacher and author George Matheson wrote: "We conquer, not in any brilliant fashion, we conquer by continuing."[21]

So don't give up—no matter what's happening to you right now. Wait patiently upon the Lord. Trust him. He knows your need. He knows the desire of your heart and your greatest hope. He is your final and more than sufficient refuge "and underneath are the everlasting arms" (Deuteronomy 33:37, KJV).

Let us not faint. Instead, setting aside all that may distract or discourage us, "Let us run with endurance the race that is set before us" (Hebrews 12:1, KJV).

Run!

April, 2012

Chapter Seven: The Pillar

"This is the church of the living God, which is the pillar and foundation of the truth."

1 TIMOTHY 3:15, NLT

"The Church's one foundation is Jesus Christ her Lord."

SAMUEL J. STONE

ℋiding in Plain Sight

We got him.

Osama Bin Laden's terror-plotting days are finally over, after nearly a decade at large.

When he was taken out by American forces in May 2011, Americans were celebrating. It's another win for the good guys and reminds us "that though the wrong seems oft so strong, God is the Ruler yet."

It's interesting how—and where—we found Osama.

Many assumed that he was running from cave to cave in the mountains, just a single step ahead of a tomahawk missile. Instead, Bin Laden had been hiding out in a mansion in Pakistan for years, according to authorities—just down the road from a military base!

He was, as one American official put it, "hiding in plain sight."

Hearing that made me wonder.

"Our neighbors? A bit strange, perhaps. They keep to themselves. But they seemed nice enough. And the tall man always smiled and waved when he came outside to get the mail."

What if Osama had cut his hair and shaved his beard, and traded in his Muslim clerical garb for a Brooks Brothers pinstripe and a red power tie? Suppose he had chosen to quietly stroll the streets of lower Manhattan carrying a brown leather briefcase?

Who would have even noticed him? Who have suspected such a quiet and polite gentleman? More importantly, who would have recognized him?

He would have been "hiding in plain sight."

Sometimes, our great mortal adversary does the same thing.

He hides in plain sight.

Paul told the Corinthians to watch out for "false apostles. They are deceitful workers who disguise themselves as apostles of Christ."

Then Paul added this:

"But I am not surprised! Even Satan disguises himself as an angel of light" (2 Corinthians 11:13, 14, NLT).

The devil has even been known to attack us through "friendly fire."

As President Warren Harding once said in exasperation over the scoundrels to whom he had given jobs:

"It's not my enemies! It's my friends who keep me pacing the floor at night!"

There's not an honest pastor who wouldn't smile at that. Well-intended and "sincerely misguided" Christians are some of the devil's most effective agents in undermining the church.

When Peter—as loyal and sincere a disciple as there was—called Jesus aside and told him, concerning his predictions of his suffering and death, "This will never happen to you!" our Savior recognized the satanic ploy. And what did he say to his beloved follower?

"Get away from me Satan! You are a dangerous trap to me" (Matthew 16:22, 23, NLT).

It must have shocked and confused Peter. After all, he meant well.

> AS WE NAVIGATE THROUGH A WORLD SATURATED WITH INFORMATION—SOME GOOD, BUT MUCH OF IT BAD, INACCURATE, AND FLAT-OUT WRONG—BELIEVERS NEED TO ASK GOD FOR THE SPIRIT OF DISCERNMENT.

As we navigate through a world saturated with information—some good, but much of it bad, inaccurate, and flat-out wrong—believers need to ask God for the spirit of discernment. Jesus promised us that the Holy Spirit would "guide you into all truth" (John 16: 13, KJV). Never has that discernment and guidance been more important than it is today.

John urges us to "test the spirits" to see if they truly are from God (1 John 4:1).

Peter tells us: "Stay alert! Watch out for your great enemy, the devil. He prowls around..." (1 Peter 5:8, NLT).

Jesus himself warns us that in these last days "many false prophets will appear and will deceive many people." They will perform "great signs and wonders, so as to deceive, if possible, even God's chosen ones—the elect!" (Matthew 24:24, NLT).

Heresy comes in many guises—even really cool ones!

And nothing sells, or draws a gullible crowd, faster than "signs and won-ders"—especially high- tech ones.

So pray daily. Study your Bible. Think.

Don't always jump on the latest bandwagon riding through town.

Remember, sometimes the devil is simply hiding in plain sight.

May, 2011

$\mathcal{L}$anguage Fit for God

The English language isn't what it used to be.

It's taken a beating.

It's easy to blame the schools. But that's a bit too convenient. Our culture has changed. It's sunk to the lowest common denominator of class and intelligence to which modern entertainment can manage to drag it. Technology has also made such breathtaking advances that we are not only a virtual society—we are an almost exclusively visual one.

People still read, but increasingly reading has been supplanted by watching. One hundred years ago, we learned about our world through books and newspapers. Today we learn through seeing and listening. Our world is smaller and the images it creates bombard us continually and instantaneously.

Even in our churches, which have always struggled to lead rather than follow, worship has been transformed by the world outside. Ever anxious to "be relevant"—whatever that really means in spiritual terms—ministers and churches have attempted to hang on to shrinking attention spans. It seems logical, then, that translations of the Bible would also reflect the desire for simple and understandable language.

If the preacher is going to say, "You know, it's like he goes, 'Cool man!' And, you know, she goes, like, 'Wow,' and then he goes, like, 'Hey man, whatever'"—then it is safe to say that the King James Version of the Bible is seriously endangered.

Which is too bad—you know?

Born in the midst of the cultural and political turmoil—and religious divisions—of the seventeenth century, the "Authorized" King James Version was the attempt of the English monarchy to offer the people a translation of the Scriptures that would unite them. The history of the most famous translation of the Bible ever penned is fascinating. What's perhaps most ironic is that the version written by William Tyndale, famed Bible translator, was the one adopted nearly wholesale by the English authorities in 1611. Why so ironic? Because Tyndale had been hounded and eventually martyred by those same authorities for his efforts to print and distribute the Bible to the masses.

England not only gave her own people a popular Bible translation, the King James Version united the whole world behind an elegant, powerful, historic, accurate, and inspiring rendition of God's Holy Word. Other than perhaps Shakespeare, there is no work of literature that has so shaped the history of western civilization. From the Pilgrims to the founders to Lincoln's masterful Second Inaugural, and to the modern eloquence of JFK and Martin Luther King, the King James Bible has profoundly impacted the story of America.

> THERE IS NO OTHER TRANSLATION OF THE BIBLE THAT EVEN COMES CLOSE TO THIS MOVING, BEAUTIFUL, AND REVERENT MASTERPIECE.

There is no other translation of the Bible—and there are many, which I employ freely—that even comes close to this moving, beautiful, and reverent masterpiece.

The King James Version of the Bible turned four hundred years old in 2011. It is sad to think that it may not survive to be five hundred. We abandon tradition with an almost cavalier dismissal. New is great. Old is bad. New is cool. Old is, well, dated.

I remember listening to one of my favorite preachers publicly read a modern translation of Isaiah 53 at an otherwise dignified Good Friday service. It didn't work—not for me. One of the first Scriptures I memorized as a child of eight was Isaiah 53:6. And I memorized it—as I did all Scripture—in the hauntingly beautiful prose of the King James:

"All we like sheep have gone astray; we have turned every one to his own way; and the Lord hath laid on him the iniquity of us all."

What cadence!

God bless many of these other helpful versions. I preach from them. Then I often tell my congregation:

"Now here's what the King James says."

For me, it is almost the final authority. I cherish it. I trust it. It has stood up to every test of time. I would hate to be without it.

Is there anything more meaningful or beautiful than "The Lord is my shepherd, I shall not want"?

Or, "And now abideth faith, hope, charity, these three; but the greatest of these is charity"?

Or "Our Father, which art in heaven"?

When the desperate man in a hotel room opened the pages of "the Good Book," he found these words written:

"For God so loved the world that he gave his only begotten Son, that whosoever believeth in him should not perish, but have everlasting life."

I love the King James. It is language befitting our sovereign God.

October, 2011

Irv's Good Advice

Irv Gordon pays careful attention to details.

He doesn't miss a thing. He's conscientious, he's disciplined, he's steadfast, and he's faithful. He takes responsibility seriously. He stays on schedule. His life is orderly. He's plainspoken.

Irv Gordon is fastidious.

I've never met Irv and probably never will. He lives in Long Island, New York. And although I don't know him, I think I know some things about him. Sometimes you can extrapolate a lot about a person from what little that's been said.

Irv Gordon is a retired schoolteacher. That tells me something about him.

But this is the thing that speaks volumes: Irv drives a 1966 Volvo that is closing in on three million miles. That's right, three million!

Wow!

I don't know about meeting Irv, but I'd sure love to see that forty-six-year old Volvo! I love old cars, always have. Along with my good friends Tom Heermans and Doug Pedersen, I go to old car shows and always have a blast (my wife thinks my infatuation borders on sickness). I've seen a lot of old beauties, but I can't ever recall seeing a car with three million miles on it.

Irv Gordon made the news with his Volvo. He was asked what the secret was to its incredible longevity.

Irv's answer?

"Read the owner's manual, and do what it says."

That's sound and simple advice. It's what Irv has done—faithfully—and it's led to reliable transportation and a long life for his Volvo.

That's good spiritual advice too.

God's Word—the Bible—is our owner's manual for life. If we would receive God's blessing and guidance, then we need to read the Bible and we need to do what it says.

One might think that this would be self-evident. In practice, however, it's a bit more complicated. As church after church—and denomination after denomination—abandons the authority of the Scriptures, more and more people struggle with the contradiction between what the Bible says and what they'd really like to do. For example, the institution of marriage—as a sacred bond and lifetime commitment in the eyes of God—has become quite negotiable. In the whole realm of personal morality, popular culture is increasingly trumping the Bible.

Even within the church.

Some evangelical leaders, in their haste to be "relevant," are exchanging what the Bible says for what culture likes. Dr. Tony Jones, the former National Coordinator of the Emergent Village Church Movement, opened an Internet conversation recently by stating that homosexuality should be "blessed" by the Christian church.

> ON THE TURBULENT SEAS OF CULTURAL REBELLION, THE BIBLE IS OUR ONLY SURE COMPASS. IT IS OUR ONLY LIGHT TO GET US TO SHORE.

We are living in the closing chapter of history. Paul warns us that "the time will come when men will not put up with sound doctrine. Instead, to suit their own desires, they will gather around them a great number of teachers to say what their itching ears want to hear" (2 Timothy 4:3, NIV). The religious community in America is filling up with "itching ears."

Despite the times—perhaps because of them—Christians who want to know how to live must read, believe, and obey the living and unchanging Word of God. The Bible was, and is, and will forever be the only standard for faith and practice for the follower of Jesus Christ.

On the turbulent seas of cultural rebellion, the Bible is our only sure compass. It is our only light to get us to shore.

Pastor Francis Chan has correctly stated that the crying need of the church today is to embrace a "higher view of God." This is only achievable through embracing a higher view of God's Word.

Paul says the Bible is the "Sword of the Spirit" and includes it as a vital weapon in the Christian's spiritual armor. We are well-armed with God's Word. Without it we are cast defenseless before the opinions of people.

Irv Gordon is right: "Read the owner's manual, and do what it says."

September, 2010

*Wh*o Needs It?

"**O**rganized religion."

The words drop from the mouth in a cynical sneer. They conjure up the facade of adults sitting in church pretending to worship. They recall the despised memories of coerced church attendance that bored us in our youth.

We don't like it. We don't want it. And we don't need it.

And so we just don't go.

"But what about your children?"

"We let them decide."

Such a deal! I only wish that offer had been around when I was ten.

Every reliable study on the planet tells us that church attendance is on the decline, and has been for years—in America and throughout the West. One recent survey revealed that only 19 percent of Americans regularly attend church. If current trends continue, as low as it is today, church attendance will be half as much in the year 2050.

We are abandoning church in droves.

One of the most popular videos on YouTube—with more than six million views—is called "Why I Hate Religion, But Love Jesus." Book titles such as *They Like Jesus But Not the Church* and *Love Jesus, Hate the Church* reinforce the impression—and the trend.

Never mind that Jesus started the church, called it "my church," and promised to build it so securely that even "the gates of hell shall not prevail against it." Increasingly, people are taking Jesus—in some informal, casual way—but leaving his church behind.

This must be said clearly and incontrovertibly: you cannot love Jesus and hate the church. It is a contradiction of devotion that leaves the heart and life forever divided. It is a lie of the devil.

> THIS MUST BE SAID CLEARLY AND INCONTROVERTIBLY: YOU CANNOT LOVE JESUS AND HATE THE CHURCH.

There are three major cultural forces driving the decline in church attendance. Each of them grows out of the wisdom of this world and not from the wisdom of God.

1. Increasing secularism. We don't want the church. As moral standards collapse, the church seems ever more distant—quaintly removed from the popular thinking of our postmodern age. It's almost an embarrassment to admit we attend church on Sundays. The world is not only too much with us —it's too much in us. And, tragically, the world is too much in the church— to the point where any thoughtful person may be justified in asking, "Why bother? I can watch TV anytime I want." As the church has become less sacred, it has become more irrelevant.

2. Increasing isolationism. We don't need the church. We have grown more proudly independent—of God and of each other. Our lives are crowded. We've permitted things and pleasures and activities and events to push the church out of our lives. So long as things are going well for us, the Sunday morning inconvenience of church is dispensable.

3. Increasing consumerism. We don't buy the church. "To what can I compare this generation?" Jesus asked. "It is like children playing a game in the public square. They complain to their friends: 'We played wedding songs, and you didn't dance, so we played funeral songs, and you didn't mourn'" (Matthew 11:16, 17, NLT). Jesus sounded frustrated with those who found it easier to raise expectations and to offer criticism rather than offer obedience. Church attendees are treated today as customers shopping around. "Show me what you've got," they say. "Show me your product—God—and if I like it, maybe I'll buy it. But you better make the pitch good—because I'm pretty particular about what I'm looking for."

How have we managed to miss the whole point of going to church? How did we invert the purpose of it?

We don't go to church to get—we go to give. We give our worship, our prayers, our fellowship, our offerings, our love, and our devotion. We give of our time and our service. We go to church not only because it may change or bless or help us in some way—but also because our presence may help or bless or change someone else. We go to church not because it is convenient— it hardly ever is—but because it is a command of God. And so it is a sin not to go.

You can get to heaven by yourself, but that's not the best way to travel there.

Here's some sound advice: "And let us not neglect our meeting together, as some people do, but encourage one another, especially now that the day of his return is drawing near" (Hebrews 10:25, NLT).

"The Bible knows nothing of solitary religion," said John Wesley.

Church—who needs it? We all do.

May, 2012

$\mathscr{S}$elling for Stew

M y father-in-law comes in handy.
He's an unofficial researcher for me!

Recently, he brought by an article that was in that day's *Dallas Morning News*. Written by Rob Dreher, the article was a well-presented and thoughtful exploration of the implications of a hot-off-the-press book entitled *American Grace: How Religion Divides and Unites Us.*[22]

A summary of his analysis is that while "American Grace" may rightfully celebrate the religious diversity and tolerance which today largely reflect post-modern American thinking, there is a grave danger in this new acceptance. The danger is that by embracing tolerance, we are surrendering theological conviction.

Dreher notes that for those to whom religion is nothing more than a set of options and opinions, theology is "not such a big deal." But, he argues, if religion is really about the eternal and binding truths concerning God and man, "then a great deal depends on maintaining theological continuity and integrity."[23]

Dreher cites a disturbing study by sociologist Christian Smith of the religious views of American youth. Smith discovered, perhaps not surprisingly, that one word may describe the response of the young to the ancient faith for which their forebears gave their lives:

"Whatever."

Smith calls this attitude—which is hardly limited to our youth—a "Moralistic Therapeutic Deism," which is "centrally about feeling good, happy, secure, at peace. It is about attaining subjective well-being, being able to resolve problems ["How To" books glut our Christian bookstores] and getting along amiably with other people."[24]

That sounds like: "I'm OK—You're OK".

A commentator who likes this new thinking, Damon Linker, says of it:

"Theologically speaking, this watered-down, anemic, insipid form of Judeo-Christianity is pretty repulsive. But politically speaking", it's "perfectly suited to serve as the civil religion of the highly differentiated 21st century United States."[25]

Postmodernism hates the arrogance of certainty. So evangelical pastor Brian McLaren suggested that we should not say anything bad about homosexuality for five years, just to see if we'd have a change of heart and become more enlightened on the matter.

> MANY PULPITS IN THIS COUNTRY HAVE JETTISONED THE BIBLICAL EXPOSITION OF ESSENTIAL DOCTRINES IN FAVOR OF POPULAR PSYCHOLOGY. OFFENDING WITH DOGMA IS A DANGEROUS THING.

There are plenty of other signs, mostly seen in the so-called emergent church movement and among mega-churches across the nation, that Christians and their leaders have not just been intimidated by the spirit of our age; we have succumbed to it.

I launched a series of Christmas messages on "The Cosmic Christ" because I'm concerned that we have attempted to tame and domesticate the King of kings so he will fit neatly into the dominant pluralistic worldview of our times. And because many pulpits in this country have jettisoned the biblical exposition of essential doctrines in favor of popular psychology. Offending with dogma is a dangerous thing.

We marvel at how Esau could have been so shortsighted to have sold his precious birthright for a bowl of stew. But his brother Jacob, who, for all his deceptive tendencies, understood the true value of things, tempted Esau to sacrifice the permanent upon the altar of the immediate. Jacob knew what mattered. Esau didn't. "What good is a birthright if I starve to death?" "What good is doctrine—what good is truth—if we can't build the new campus?"

So Esau got his stomach filled. In exchange, Jacob gained the eternal promise and blessing of Jehovah. Esau "ate and drank, and rose up and went his way. Thus Esau scorned his birthright as beneath his notice" (Genesis 25:34, Amplified Bible).

As Rob Dreher reminds us, there's quite a bit at stake in all this faith and theology business.

Jim Elliot, who gave his life as a young missionary in the jungles of South America in 1956, wrote: "He is no fool who gives up what he cannot keep to gain that which he cannot lose." That's something to keep in mind the next time we're tempted to sell our spiritual and theological heritage for a bowl of postmodern stew.

December, 2010

The Tapestry

Howard Snitzer is alive today because of teamwork.

When the fifty-four-year-old collapsed on a freezing sidewalk in Minnesota, three people came running to help him. Two of them were auto mechanics, the other a high school teacher.

For the next hour and a half, more than twenty-five additional people took turns performing CPR on Snitzer until a rescue helicopter took him to the hospital.

Howard Snitzer made it because men and women came together.

No one person could have done it alone. Everyone needed each other— and Howard Snitzer needed them all. Dr. Bruce Wilkoff called it "remarkable. It's a great example of people doing the right thing and having it work out."

It's also a great example of people working together. Howard Snitzer had a great need. In agreeing to team up, in agreeing to cooperate, in agreeing to come together for a great common cause, more than two dozen people were able to do something truly and literally life-changing.

This is the meaning of Christian community—coming together to make a difference in the lives of others.

This past weekend, our small church had a couple of awesome services: Good Friday and then Easter. People came, they worshiped, and for a while they shared their lives with others in something significant. In doing this together, they were blessed, inspired, and encouraged.

It was beautiful and it was special.

Then it was over.

Everyone left and went their separate ways to lead their separate lives.

Like every church, we'd love to see them all return next Sunday. But like every church, we know that probably won't happen. Easter comes but once a year. And all of us think, "Wouldn't it be nice if every week was like today?"

It could be—if we all realized how important it is for us to come together—consistently and regularly, and if we shared our lives and our needs in corporate worship. It could be—if we all understood the importance of community.

It could be if we all remembered that after declaring everything "good," God issued his first negative: "It is not good for the man to be alone" (Genesis 2:18).

I remember touring a juvenile detention facility during my years with Prison Fellowship. Across one wall, the young residents had painted a large and colorful mural. It was an acrostic for the word *Team*: "Together Everyone Achieves More."

There is a richness and fullness and completeness in the beautiful tapestry of togetherness.

When the church began in Jerusalem, the book of Acts records that "all the believers met together in one place and shared everything they had." They "shared the money," they "worshiped together," "met in homes," and they "shared their meals" (Acts 2:44-46, NLT).

It was this strong and inviolate bond of community that helped to make this first church impregnable against all manner of persecution, oppression, and suffering.

Thirty-five times in the New Testament two words appear together: "one another." We are told to "comfort one another," "forgive one another," "accept one another" and, above all else, to "love one another."

John Wesley was right: "The Bible knows nothing of a solitary religion." The apostle Paul told the believers at Philippi, "We are in this struggle together" (Philippians 1:30, NLT).

Yes, we are.

We were made for each other. We need each other. You and I were made for community. This is the way God meant it to be.

G. K. Chesterton wrote: "We are all in the same boat in a stormy sea, and we owe each other a terrible loyalty."[26]

Go back to church this Sunday. You need the people there—and they all need you.

You're part of a divine tapestry.

> GO BACK TO CHURCH THIS SUNDAY. YOU NEED THE PEOPLE THERE—AND THEY ALL NEED YOU.

Howard Snitzer could tell you that in coming together, you might make a big difference in somebody's life.

April, 2011

$\mathscr{B}$rightly Colored Cereal Balls

D id you hear about the woman in San Diego who sued Cap'n Crunch? She had purchased a box of Cap'n Crunch with Crunchberries because she believed that the "crunchberries" were real fruit. When she discovered, to her great dismay, that they were, in fact, brightly colored cereal balls, the woman decided to sue General Mills, the makers. She alleged the cereal company had perpetrated a fraud.

The woman admitted she'd been eating Cap'n Crunch with Crunchberries for four years before she discovered that the cereal balls were not real fruit. She argued that she was intentionally deceived. A federal judge in California thought she should have known better. Case dismissed.

Imagine. For four years, this woman didn't know the difference between brightly colored cereal balls and real fruit! And when she finally realized the truth, she wanted to blame someone else. But we shouldn't be too hard on this poor deceived soul. There are a whole lot of professing Christians in this country who are munching on brightly colored cereal balls and mistaking them for real fruit. Day after day. Week after week. Sunday after Sunday. And some of them have been doing this for a lot longer than four years.

Charles Colson once said that the church in America was "five miles wide and five inches deep." There is a genuine crisis of spiritual understanding—a crisis of depth and maturity—in the church today. Thousands are being deceived, not by a cereal company, but by popular "faith teachers" who are encouraging naïve believers to substitute instant, pain-free gratification and success for the steady spiritual growth, self-denial, and perseverance of the saints—God as a celestial bellhop.

> THERE IS A GENUINE CRISIS OF SPIRITUAL UNDERSTANDING—A CRISIS OF DEPTH AND MATURITY—IN THE CHURCH TODAY.

Part of this is the fault of an infiltrating popular culture that has dulled our moral sensitivities and shamed our convictions into silence. Part of this crisis is caused by the temper of our times.

This is nothing less than prophetic. Jesus himself said that in the last days, because of pervasive evil, "the love of many will grow cold" (Matthew 24:12, NLT). Paul warned Timothy that "the time is coming when people will no longer listen to sound and wholesome teaching. They will follow their own desires and will look for teachers who will tell them whatever their itching ears want to hear. They will reject the truth and chase after myths" (2 Timothy 4:3, 4, NLT). This crisis is at least aided and abetted by the church's temptation to do—and say—just about anything to get the attention of a postmodern world.

While we are told this is how it would be in the closing days of history, it is hardly new. Paul told the Corinthians that "I couldn't talk to you as I would to spiritual people. I had to talk as though you still belonged to this world. Or as though you were infants in the Christian life. I had to feed you with milk, not with solid food, because you weren't ready for anything stronger" (1 Corinthians 3:1, 2, NLT).

The only way you and I can live the true Christian life in this deceptive and dangerous world is to be "growing in every way more and more like Christ," as Paul encouraged the Ephesians (Ephesians 4:15, NLT). We must persevere in our Christian maturity and growth. The writer of Hebrews tells us that "someone who lives on milk is still an infant and doesn't know how to do what is right. Solid food is for those who are mature, who through training have the skill to recognize the difference between right and wrong" (Hebrews 5:13, 14, NLT).

This is called discernment.

It's the ability to know the difference between brightly colored cereal balls and real fruit.

July, 2009

Our Father

There is no greater feeling in all the world than when she runs delightedly into my arms.

Ava is my nearly two-year-old granddaughter. I try my best to be circumspect around others, but I love her more than can be told and I love being a grandfather! I could never fully appreciate the bumper sticker that confesses: "I should have had grandchildren first!"

Now I better understand.

Ava is my "little toadstool." (I know: "OK, enough of that already!").

Being a grandparent—and those who are know I'm right—is a job with no heavy lifting and a ton of benefits. I get to see Ava pretty much when I want, but never as much as I'd like. Perfect! I have neither extended nor fiduciary obligations that might interfere significantly with my life. I care deeply about what happens to her—her health, happiness, education, provisions, training, discipline, and all other collateral concerns. I have, however, no ultimate responsibility for any of these.

My chief duty is to entertain Ava: to offer her love, kindness, and gifts, to run around in the backyard with her, to hold her and kiss her and to feed her some (occasional) M&Ms. And to read to her and watch *Beauty and the Beast*—repeatedly. But that's OK, too; we both love that movie.

Obviously, I like my job description: all the joys of having children but none of the tough stuff.

It doesn't get any better.

Of course, Ava will need to learn right from wrong. She'll need limits. She'll need lessons. She'll need curfews. She'll need discipline. She'll need to experience some challenges so she'll be able to mature and grow into a lovely young woman. Fortunately, her parents will be there to handle nearly all of these parts, with my standby encouragement. They will comfort her, guide her, and love her through the ups and downs of growing up.

Yes, a father is different than a grandfather.

It's interesting to observe how we are sometimes tempted to view God. We pray, "Our Father." Yet we often expect God to conduct himself toward us more like a kindly old grandfather—or perhaps a happy and generous rich uncle.

C. S. Lewis framed this analogy in his book *The Problem of Pain*.

"What would really satisfy us," Lewis wrote, "would be a God who said of anything we happened to like doing, 'What does it matter so long as they are contented?' We want, in fact, not so much a Father in Heaven as a grandfather in heaven—a senile benevolence who, as they say, 'liked to see young people enjoying themselves,' and whose plan for the universe was simply that it might be said at the end of each day, 'a good time was had by all.'"

Lewis conceded that he "should very much like to live in a universe which was governed on such lines."[27]

He knew better.

The tragedy today is that so many of our churches and pulpits are filled with those who have this very false idea of God. In our egocentric, self-esteem-saturated society, the appeals to a health and wealth, pain- and problem-free gospel are very popular. We are told that we deserve abundant blessings and that God, since he loves us so much, is obligated to provide them.

This is a twisted concept of God. It is a fundamental misunderstanding of divine love.

Yes, God does bless us in so many ways. He delights in doing so, not because he's a weak and indulging deity who doesn't know when he's spoiling us, but because he is a sovereign God who is both strong and compassionate, both holy and mer-

> AS PAUL TELLS THE ROMANS, GOD IS BOTH GOOD AND SEVERE.

ciful. As Paul tells the Romans, God is both good and severe (Romans 11:22).

"The Lord disciplines those he loves," Hebrews tells us. "As you endure this divine discipline, remember that God is treating you as his own children...God's discipline is always good for us, so that we might share in his holiness" (Hebrews 12:6, 7, 10, NLT).

Earthly grandparents may have fun doting on their grandkids.

God is always "Our Father."

January, 2011

*B*ell's Hell

Pastor Rob Bell certainly means well, I'll give him that.
He's sincere and he wants people to come to know the Jesus he knows and loves. When you're the forty-something hip pastor of a ten-thousand-member contemporary church in Michigan and you have a national following among young evangelicals, what do you do to enlarge it?

You tell them that hell is a state of mind.

It's not a real place. And no loving God would ever send anyone to such a horrible doom.

You tell them that eventually everyone gets to heaven.

Then you tell them that Christ's death on the cross was a wonderful example of self-denial and a bit of "brilliant, creative work" that places "the Jesus story in language their listeners would understand."

Say again?

Bell is clearly uncomfortable with the hymn writer's "Old, Old Story" of redemption. So he's decided to update it along lines that his postmodern hearers will find more palatable. This includes relegating God to a well-intended and kindly deity who hopes everyone makes it in the end. Sort of like a divine Wizard of Oz. Openly wrestling with God's omnipotence and his benign desire for universal salvation, Bell asks: "Will God get what he wants?"[28]

Is Pastor Bell a Christian? I sure hope so.

But he's also a heretic.

This wouldn't be a cause for particular alarm, except that Rob Bell is also an influential evangelical Christian leader. Al Mohler, president of the Southern Baptist Theological Seminary, has described Bell's book, *Love Wins*, as "a massive tragedy by any measure."[29]

Indeed, and a sober warning as well.

You might say that this book rings out "like a bell in the night."

It is but the beginning of prophetic apostasy.

We know that in the closing days of history, the church will come under increasing attack for its orthodoxy. Many will depart from the faith. They will reject "sound doctrine," Paul says. "They will follow their own desires and will look for teachers who will tell them whatever their itching ears want to hear. They will reject the truth and chase after myths" (2 Timothy 4:3, 4, NLT).

It's hard to say what awards Pastor Bell's book may garner, but he certainly earned the 2011 "Itching Ears Award."

Of the rebellious Judah, God says through the prophet Isaiah:

"They tell the prophets, 'Don't tell us what is right. Tell us nice things. Tell us lies. Forget all this gloom. Get off your narrow path'" (Isaiah 30:10, 11, NLT).

Bell's *Love Wins* attempts to do just that.

If today's audience finds a literal and eternal hell distasteful (let's be honest, who doesn't?) then simply tell them not to worry. There isn't any. According to Bell, Christ's death was a nice thing to do, but hardly needed. Bell's universalism puts a new twist on the old hymn, "When We All Get to Heaven."

Bell at least deserves credit for recognizing that the judgmental, self-righteous God of many social activists is not the loving God of the Bible. Yes, God is love and he loves this world and he will someday redeem it fully. God's heart is filled with compassion.

> GOD'S LOVE IS SO GREAT THAT HE GAVE UP HIS ONLY SON TO THE INDESCRIBABLE TORTURE OF CALVARY IN ORDER TO SAVE US FROM HELL, NOT TO DENY ITS EXISTENCE.

But God's love is so great that he gave up his only Son to the indescribable torture of Calvary in order to save us from hell, not to deny its existence. To believe otherwise is to make the atonement quite irrelevant and beside the point. God's cruelty would be displayed not in sending anyone to hell for rejecting Christ, but in sending his Son to die a needless death.

Bell's hell and his universal salvation do not prove the love of God. They make a mockery of it.

Historian Richard Niebuhr once defined liberal theology with this withering indictment:

"A God without wrath brought men without sin into a Kingdom without judgment through Christ without a cross."[30]

Pray for Rob Bell. And pray for the church.

April, 2011

Chapter Eight: This Is Life

"Life is a little gleam of time between two eternities."
THOMAS CARLYLE

*H*onest to God

When the Transportation Security Administration installed 385 full-body scanners in sixty-eight of the nation's busiest airports, there was the predictable invasion-of-privacy outcry.

"'Don't touch my junk' is the anthem of the modern man," wrote columnist Charles Krauthammer. He labeled the enhanced procedures "a national homage to political correctness." He predicted that Americans would push back against these intrusions, and that with these measures 'you've gone too far, Big Bro.' The sleeping giant awakes."[31]

Perhaps he's right. But in the struggle to balance liberty with security, and individual privacy with the greater public interest, Americans, as much as they chafe, have made some practical accommodations. Still, it's safe (no pun intended) to say that we all prize our independence and our privacy.

When it comes to our lives we tend to let others go so far—and then no further. We reserve that private space. "Don't touch my junk!"

It can't work that way with God. He touches what he wants to.

After telling us that God's word is powerful and sharper than any two-edged sword and that it cuts between soul and spirit—right down to the very bone of our being, so to speak—the writer of Hebrews adds this:

"It exposes our innermost thoughts and desires. Nothing in all creation is hidden from God. Everything is naked and exposed before his eyes, and he is the one to whom we are accountable" (Hebrews 4:12, 13, NLT).

God's full-body, full-soul, full-mind scanner sees all our junk.

This is a fearful thing. God intends it to be. It's also incredibly comforting and reassuring.

Because the God who made us and knows us inside out is the same God who still loves us beyond anything we can imagine!

David, who had his share of "junk," wrote: "O Lord, you have examined my heart and know everything about me... I can never escape from your Spirit! I can never get away from your presence!" (Psalm 139:1, 7, NLT).

No, there's nowhere to hide from God. Not a place on the planet.

Then again, why do we need to? Why would we want to?

God is the one to whom we can flee in confidence when the world has shut us out—or we've shut out the world. The one time and place we must be honest before God is when we pray.

In his wonderful book entitled *Prayer: Does It Make Any Difference?* Philip Yancey writes:

"Prayer makes room for the unspeakable, those secret compartments of shame and regret that we seal away from the outside world." Yancey points out that trust deepens relationships.[32]

And our relationship with God will deepen as we come before him with a conscious transparency that, for God, is rather beside the point. We may do so without fear of what God thinks of us. After all, God's not just another person. He knows what we've done. He knows who we are. He knows what we are. He knows all that before we come to him. So, why not trust him with the knowledge he already has? It doesn't affect God if we are honest before him. But it does affect us.

> IT DOESN'T AFFECT GOD IF WE ARE HONEST BEFORE HIM. BUT IT DOES AFFECT US.

When we learn to trust God and his love, we'll be less inclined to fear coming before him with our true selves. C.S. Lewis, typically, said it well:

"We must lay before him what is in us, not what ought to be in us."[33]

We must bring God our junk.

When King David finally admitted that God desires "honesty from the heart," God changed David's heart. He cleansed his soul, forgave his sin, and restored his joy (Psalm 51).

When we do the same—when we are honest to God—it will change us. He will change us.

May, 2011

*O*ne More for the Gipper

They called him The Gipper.

It was a name from one of his old movies. Then again, we didn't think that anyone who acted in movies could ever be the Leader of the Free World.

But he was—twice.

And that came after being elected Governor of California—twice.

He restored America's confidence, renewed its patriotism, revitalized its economy, and led the United States to victory in the Cold War. He forged an alliance with the pope and the prime minister of England to undermine the Soviet empire, tear down the Berlin Wall, toss communism on the ash heap of history, and spread freedom throughout the world.

Not too shabby for a B-rated movie actor. But before he did all this, Ronald Wilson Reagan nearly died.

Shortly after becoming the nation's fortieth president in 1981, Mr. Reagan was shot by John Hinckley outside a Washington DC hotel, following a speaking engagement. Fortunately, Hinckley was not a very good shot. All six bullets missed the president, but the final one ricocheted off the limousine and hit Reagan underneath his raised arm, lodging about an inch from his heart. Reagan's grace under fire (quite literally) won the admiration of a country thankful for his recovery.

Years later, in her book *Angels Don't Die*, the president's daughter, Patti Davis, wrote about the assassination attempt:

"The following day my father said he knew his physical healing was directly dependent on his ability to forgive John Hinckley. By showing me that forgiveness is the key to everything, including physical health and healing, he gave me an example of Christlike thinking."[34]

Those once closest to Jesus weren't always so sure about forgiveness. They lived in harsh and unforgiving times.

Peter, not a patient man, asked him: "Lord, how often should I forgive someone who sins against me? Seven times?" That would seem a reasonable thing, from an impatient man's perspective. So Jesus must have startled Peter with his reply:

"No," he smiled, "not seven times, but seventy times seven!" (Matthew 18:21, 22, NLT).

That's a whole lot of forgiving. And practically speaking, who would keep track?

"Forgiveness is the key to everything."

Jesus thought so. He told us that we could "pray for anything, and if you believe that you've received it, it will be yours." That's quite a promise. But then he added a caveat:

"But when you are praying, first forgive anyone you are holding a grudge against, so that your Father in heaven will forgive your sins too" (Mark 11:24, 25, NLT). The inference drawn is what Jesus states bluntly in his Sermon on the Mount in Matthew 6:

"If you forgive those who sin against you, your heavenly Father will forgive you. But if you refuse to forgive others, your Father will not forgive your sins" (vs. 15, NLT).

> FORGIVENESS REALLY IS THAT IMPORTANT. IN FACT, IT'S PARAMOUNT. GOD FORGIVES; JESUS FORGAVE; WE MUST FORGIVE.

Forgiveness really is that important. In fact, it's paramount. God forgives; Jesus forgave; we must forgive.

Jesus says that even if we get to church and are ready to place our offering in the plate and then remember that things are not right with someone else, we must drop everything and "go and be reconciled to that person. Then come and offer your sacrifice to God" (Matthew 5:23, 24, NLT).

Forgiveness—offering it, and sometimes receiving it—is not always easy. But we don't get to heaven without it. Forgiveness is essential to our lives. And our health, our happiness, and our joy.

If nothing strengthens our faith like suffering, it may also be said that nothing more beautifully displays our faith like forgiveness. It led one daughter to observe of her father: "By showing me that forgiveness is the key to everything… he gave me an example of Christlike thinking."

It was one more win for The Gipper.

February, 2011

$\mathscr{P}$recarious

They never intended to die.

They were out to have a great time. It was a day trip with family and friends.

They just ignored the sign.

Three young people in their twenties were hiking in California's Yosemite National Park when they climbed the steep and slippery Mist Trail until they reached Vernal Fall. It is one of Yosemite's most popular and spectacular waterfalls.

There was a metal guardrail. It had been placed there by park authorities to keep visitors away from the swift-moving water of the Merced River. Just twenty-five feet from the precipice of the fall, the young people crossed over the guardrail and entered the water. Other hikers who were there kept telling them, "It's not safe!"

They paid no attention.

There had been a near-record Sierra snow pack the previous winter and a cool rainy spring. The Merced River was raging. When one of the hikers slipped, another reached for her. When he went into the water, the third hiker tried to grab him, and then he too slipped into the river.

Caught in the current, the three hikers were swept to their deaths 317 feet below.

A single sign warns hikers not to cross the guardrail or to swim in the pools near the fall. They ignored the sign. They ignored other hikers attempting to warn them of the danger. Vernal Fall is beautiful. To get in the waters of the Merced River is a temptation. It is also very perilous.

Kurt Repanshek, editor of the National Parks Traveler website, commented after the tragedy: "While there are railings and signs in some of the more dangerous spots, those often are ignored by more than a few visitors, to their detriment."

Is this not equally valid in the spiritual realm?

The psalmist writes about those who insist on ignoring God and going their own way, morally and spiritually:

"Truly, you put them on a slippery path and send them sliding over the cliff to destruction. In an instant they are destroyed, completely swept away by terrors" (Psalm 73:18, 19, NLT).

> THE NARROW ROAD OF CHRISTIAN FAITH MAY SOMETIMES BE DIFFICULT AND LONELY TO TRAVEL, BUT IT GIVES US SAFE PASSAGE TO A HAPPY END.

It may be a broad and popular highway that the world travels, but Jesus says that it leads not to life and safety, but to destruction (Matthew 7:13). "There is a path before each person that seems right, but it ends in death" (Proverbs 16:25, NLT).

The apostle Paul warns us: "If you think you are standing strong, be careful not to fall" (1 Corinthians 10:12, NLT).

In a world filled with danger and temptation, God has promised his people guidance and protection. But these are premised on our allegiance to his standards and our obedience to his commands. The narrow road of Christian faith may sometimes be difficult and lonely to travel, but it gives us safe passage to a happy end.

But we must read and follow the signs.

God has given us his Word, the Bible, as a lamp to guide our feet and a light for our path (Psalm 119:105). We must read it, study it, know it, and follow it. We must heed its warnings, live by its precepts, and claim its promises.

And what will God do? He will keep us safe.

Jude tells us that God is "able to keep you from falling" (vs. 24, KJV).

In her beautiful prayer of praise, Hannah rejoices that God "will guard the feet of his saints" (1 Samuel 2:9). God will catch us; he'll support us, strengthen us, and encourage us.

And the psalmist's testimony will be our own: "I cried out 'I am slipping', but your unfailing love, O Lord, supported me. When doubts filled my mind, your comfort gave me renewed hope and cheer" (Psalm 94:18, 19, NLT).

If you and I will remain inside the guardrail of God's Word—if we will obey his commands and live by his standards—then God will keep us safely inside the railing of his love, grace, and protection.

Anything less would be precarious.

November, 2011

$\mathcal{J}$alloh's Job

You normally wouldn't expect to find much virtue in a New York City cab.

Fortunately for John James, he picked the right one.

James jumped out of his taxi and, as he watched it speed away, suddenly realized he'd forgotten something. And not just anything. In the backseat he had left a bag containing jewelry and cash. Total worth: $100,000.

It might have been an expensive memory lapse.

"I thought that it was the end of the world," James said.

But while he had forgotten his valuables, he did have something even more precious: his taxi receipt. He managed to track down the driver.

At this point in the story, you might expect a disappointing end. ("Bag? What bag?"). But Zubiru Jalloh, the cab driver who lives in Brooklyn, had indeed found the bag in his backseat. What's amazing is what he did with it. He kept it safe. He waited for Mr. James to claim it.

How easy it would have been to do otherwise—and how tempting. For a Brooklyn cabbie, that was a lot of money. You can't expect a hundred grand just to sit in the backseat of a cab unattended in New York City! Who would ever have known? After all, this wasn't really stealing, was it? John James was a careless fool for forgetting the bag. And one man's forgetfulness is another man's gain, right?

That's not how Zubiru Jalloh saw it. He explained:

"This is my job—to be honest and truthful to people."

"My job"?

Yes, and something more too: "That's exactly what my religion told me." And because of his "religion," Zubiru Jolloh reluctantly accepted $1,000 as a reward instead of taking $100,000 that wasn't his.

What is our "job" as Christians? How honest are we? What does our "religion" tell us about honesty? How willing are we to cut corners when it comes to being "honest and truthful to people?"

Job said that he would maintain a clear conscience for as long as he lived (Job 27:6).

King David, in repenting of his dishonesty, acknowledged in his prayer: "You desire honesty from the heart" (Psalm 51:6, NLT).

The Old Testament has much to say about maintaining honest weights and measures in business transactions. "A false balance is abomination to the Lord; but a just weight is his delight" (Proverbs 11:1, KJV).

The challenge facing Christians in this postmodern age is that honesty as a virtue has often fallen prey to the practical accommodations of advancing one's interests. We've seen it on Wall Street, and, as always, we've seen plenty of it in politics. We've also seen it in the church.

Honesty has also taken a hit in our homes, our marriages, our schools, and our colleges.

Like a slow-moving and undetected cancer, dishonesty eats away at the vitality of our social institutions and community life. Because we are increasingly surrounded by cheating and lying and exploitation, we are in danger of being morally anesthetized. Our virtue is at risk of being seduced by the attractive pitchmen of greed and selfishness.

> DISHONESTY ALWAYS HIDES. IT ALWAYS TEMPTS. AND IT IS ALWAYS SUBTLE. DISHONESTY IS A GREAT TALKER AND CAN BE VERY PERSUASIVE.

Dishonesty always hides. It always tempts. And it is always subtle. Dishonesty is a great talker and can be very persuasive.

Jesus told us to let the light of our lives and our character so shine before others that they might see our virtue by the way we live–by our conduct. And that God would receive glory by the way we lived (Matthew 5:16).

The apostle Paul told us to pursue those things that are honest and just—honest things, not only in the sight of the Lord, but also in the sight of men" (2 Corinthians 8:21).

This is our duty as believers—to live worthy of our calling in Jesus Christ—every day and in every way.

Zubiru Jalloh would say that honesty is our "job."

March 2011

_The Dummy in Shades

Kathleen Frascinella must have been in a real hurry to get somewhere. She got pulled over on the Long Island Expressway for driving in the high occupancy vehicle lane. She did have another passenger—an elaborately attired dummy! You've got to hand it to Kathleen. She went to great lengths to perpetrate this deception and should get high marks for creativity and a fine sense of humor.

She made one mistake, however.

The police officer who caught her became suspicious when he noticed the dummy was wearing sunglasses. You see, it was a cloudy day.

Just as we must be impressed with Kathleen's ingenuity, this officer is even more impressive for his masterful attention to detail and keen observation skills. After all, for him this wasn't a plot invested with careful planning; it was an instantaneous reaction based on an otherwise easily missed minor detail.

This guy should be a detective; he makes Colombo look like an amateur!

It's truly amazing that with all those vehicles traveling on the Long Island Expressway that overcast day, this policeman was alert enough to notice that dummy wearing those sunglasses, connect it with the weather, and make the instant decision to pursue.

How would you like to be this guy's teenage daughter? No dummy in shades is going to trick him! He doesn't miss anything.

Neither does God.

Sometimes, just like Kathleen, we prop up a spiritual dummy in sunglasses and we think God won't notice. But he always does. Nothing gets by God.

When the reality of God's omniscience occurs to us, it can often seem like the Christmas song: "He knows if you've been bad or good, so be good for goodness' sake!" The scriptures are forthright in this regard:

"Nothing in all creation is hidden from God. Everything is naked and exposed before his eyes, and he is the one to whom we are accountable" (Hebrews 4:13, NLT).

Yet this stark reality is not just convicting. It is also very comforting.

"O Lord, you have examined my heart," David cries, "and you know everything about me." After spending the rest of the beautiful 139th Psalm cataloging God's intimate knowledge, David concludes: "How precious are your thoughts about me." He invites God to search him, know him, and test him and then to show him how he ought to live (Psalm 139:21-24).

God doesn't just see our sin. He sees our struggles. He knows our fears and our doubts; he knows our hopes and he sees our remorse. He knows our intentions and our motives. He knows when we rise to the occasion and he knows when we stumble and fall. He not only knows what we've tried to do but failed; he also knows what we need to do and will help. He understands fully the noble and good ambitions of our hearts. And he knows how weak we really are without him.

> WE'RE NOT FREE TO SIN BUT WE ARE SET FREE FROM SIN. AND WHILE GOD'S GRACE MUST NEVER BE PRESUMED, IT IS ALWAYS MORE THAN SUFFICIENT

Is there anyone else we'd sooner trust with this awareness?

God not only convicts us, he comforts us. He's not just a judge; God is also a friend, a guide, and an encourager. Since he knows everything about us, he also knows our longings. He knows that we want to be something that in this life and this world we can never be: perfect.

And that's where God's grace comes in.

We're not free to sin but we are set free from sin. And while God's grace must never be presumed, it is always more than sufficient: it is abounding. Even—and especially—when we sin.

While we may find it difficult to be our true selves before others, even with those who know us best, we are never anything else with God. It's rather silly to try and pretend before God to be something that God and I both know I'm not. Gods shakes his head at our play-acting. He forgives even our vain attempts to deceive him.

If there's one person I need to trust as an "accountability partner," it's Jesus.

Can we hide from God? Do we really need to?

Don't be a dummy.

November, 2010

*P*eppers and the Power of God

Edmund McIlhenny was a hardworking businessman. Before the Civil War, he owned a sugar plantation and salt works on Avery Island, Louisiana. When the war came, he had to escape the onslaught of Northern troops invading the area. When he returned to his plantation at the war's end in 1865, McIlhenny found nothing but devastation and ruin. His beloved plantation, like so many others, had been destroyed.

But he did notice one small sign of life amidst the ruins. A few Mexican peppers had somehow managed to re-seed themselves in the kitchen garden. With little to eat, McIlhenny began to experiment. He started grinding the hot peppers to make a sauce that would spice up his bland and dreary diet. He liked the taste.

Today, we call it Tabasco. Edmund McIlhenny's family still runs the company.

Hope—and all that he cherished—seemed lost to Edmund McIlhenny when he came back to what he once called home. All that was most familiar was gone forever. It's hard to imagine that he ever thought that a new and exciting thing was about to spring forth from the ashes of his personal devastation.

How could he believe that the best was yet to come? How could he have guessed that from this tragedy of war and destruction, his greatest triumph would yet emerge? How could Edmund McIlhenny have possibly imagined that his dark valley of despair would be the means to lead him to a pinnacle of prosperity and success?

He didn't know. He couldn't have imagined it in his wildest dreams.

In a different yet still similar way, God has often used personal tragedies and trials in people's lives to be an inspiration and incredible ministry to countless others. When a teenager named Joni Eareckson dove into the water and broke her neck, she had no idea that God would someday use her accident as an inspiration to the faith of so many. When her parents discovered that her world was enclosed by silent darkness, they had no idea that Helen Keller would someday become a worldwide symbol of hope to millions.

Through the prophet Isaiah, God said to Israel that what he had already done in choosing this small nation as his own "is nothing compared to what I am going to do. For I am about to do something new... Do you not see it? I will make a pathway through the wilderness. I will create rivers in the dry wasteland... I have made Israel for myself, and they will someday honor me before the whole world" (Isaiah 43:18-21, NLT).

For so many of us it sometimes seems, especially in these uncertain days, that no river of hope could ever flow through the dry wasteland of our defeat or despair or heartache. That there can be no pathway through our personal wilderness. But Jesus reminds us that the things that are impossible with man are very possible with God. And it was Paul, quoting Isaiah to the Corinthians, who declared that "no eye has seen, no ear has heard and no mind has imagined what God has prepared for those who love him" (1 Corinthians 2:9, NLT).

> ## GOD CAN DO ANYTHING. AND HE CAN USE ANYTHING.

Yes, we must never forget, no matter what our personal situation may be—no matter what crisis we're facing—that our mighty and gracious God is able to accomplish far beyond anything we could hope or think possible.

God can do anything. And he can use anything.

Even a few Mexican pepper plants growing in a kitchen. Unplanted by human hands.

August, 2009

_R_eading the Obits

It may be part of my lifelong love affair with biography and history, but I enjoy reading obituaries. People fascinate me, so do their lives. Perhaps this enjoyment of obituaries is part, too, of my youthful interest in the funeral business. I seriously considered becoming an undertaker at one time and thought it would be a wonderful and unique way to share my faith. My family still doesn't fully appreciate that.

In the fifth chapter of Genesis, there is a lengthy list of obituaries. We can't tell much from the list of names, just ages and who they "begat." But buried (no pun intended!) right in the middle of that list is the name of Enoch. It says that he was the father of Methuselah. This is a minor claim to fame, since Methuselah lived longer than anyone ever lived on earth—969 years.

But then we read a much more interesting sentence: "Enoch walked with God; then he was no more, because God took him away" (Genesis 5:24, NIV). In fact, it mentions this twice, about Enoch walking with God, once in verse 22 and then again in verse 24.

The fact that he "walked with God" got Enoch included in the "faith chapter" of Hebrews 11. It says that Enoch "was commended as one who pleased God"(Hebrews 11:5, NIV).

Walking with God. Pleasing God. That's quite a tribute. I can't think of anything more important in our lives. I can't think of a greater or more noble ambition. I can't think of a finer commendation than to have it be said of you and of me: "She walked with God." "He pleased God." Nothing should matter more to us. There is no greater measure of a man's life than his relationship with God. All else pales by comparison.

To commune with God so closely, to love God so dearly, to reflect the mind and temperament of Jesus Christ so completely as to be known as one who "walks with God."

> THERE IS NO GREATER MEASURE OF A MAN'S LIFE THAN HIS RELATIONSHIP WITH GOD.

Is there any higher priority or aim in life than this? Can any achievement come close?

I've thought of writing my own obituary well in advance, so all the facts and achievements of my life are duly noted. But rather than that bit of final self-promotion, I'd rather have my wife and my daughters and my grandchildren (and my friends, if there are any still around) say of me simply this, and mean it: "He walked with God."

I have a good friend who told me recently that "the dash" speaks volumes. I was puzzled, so he explained. On most tombstones and in most biographies, there is a date of birth and a date of death. In between those dates, there is a dash. That simple dash signifies the life lived between those dates. I thought about that. And I recalled the many times I've walked in cemeteries (another death-related interest!), seeing the years chiseled on the headstones and wondering about all that took place between those two dates.

The prophet Micah summed it up quite well:

"He has showed you, O man, what is good, and what does the Lord require of you? To act justly and to love mercy and to walk humbly with your God" (Micah 6:8, NIV)

Sounds like a pretty good obit to me.

March, 2009

So What?

Watchman Nee had it about right.

The great early twentieth-century Chinese Christian leader and author said of the Christian faith:

"Show the world Christianity and the world will oppose it vigorously. Show the world the fruits of Christianity and it will applaud."[35]

Nee argued that the watching world must render a clear verdict on Christian belief and its practical implications, either for or against.

In an article published in *USA Today*, Cathy Lynn Grossman wrote about the growing disconnect between faith and life. Increasingly, Grossman said, people are not so much atheists—which actually honors the importance of faith as a philosophical construct—as they are simply apathetic about religion.[36]

Many Americans just don't care. It doesn't matter. Spiritual considerations are quite beside the point of daily life.

In a survey on religious attitudes, 46 percent of respondents said they never wonder whether they will go to heaven. Forty-four percent said they never spend time seeking "eternal wisdom." And over a fourth of those surveyed—28 percent—said, "It's not a major priority in my life to find my deeper purpose."

In the discussion over God, religion, and atheism, wrote Grossman, the present drift seems to be toward an attitude that she summed up as, "So what?"[37]

Surprising?

Watchman Nee, who spent the last twenty years of his life in a Chinese prison because of his faith in Christ, wouldn't think so. If it is shown neither Christianity nor its fruits, Nee would argue that the world would neither vigorously oppose nor applaud the Christian faith. Instead, it would ignore it. This is the most ignominious of all rejections. In the secular postmodern era in which we live, Christianity has been neutered—sidelined to irrelevance by too many of us who do not understand it, cannot explain it, and do not live it.

The world is winning the battle for our hearts and minds. Popular culture is playing the fiddle and sadly the church is dancing to its tune.

C.S. Lewis, who eloquently stated the case for an integrated Christianity that consistently impacted all of life, wrote that "one thing Christianity cannot be is moderately important."[38]

A man named James, the brother of Jesus Christ, wrote a letter two thousand years ago that forcefully made this same central claim. While Martin Luther famously dismissed the book of James as "an epistle of straw" because he felt it treated salvation by faith too lightly, James insisted—with forthright common sense and honesty—that our faith must have consequences. It must guide the way we live our lives every day.

> THE FRUITS OF CHRISTIANITY MUST BE PLANTED AND GROWN IN THE HEART AND MIND OF THE BELIEVER, HARVESTED IN THE LIFE, AND SHOWN TO THE WORLD.

"But don't just listen to God's word," James wrote. "You must do what it says. Otherwise, you are only fooling yourselves... faith by itself isn't enough. Unless it produces good deeds, it is dead and useless" (James 1:22; 2:17, NLT).

Those are strong words.

Whether addressing temptation and sin, trust and doubt, wealth and poverty, prejudice and favoritism, or gossip and presumption, James drove home his point that believing cannot be separated from behaving in the life of the true follower of Jesus Christ. The fruits of Christianity must be planted and grown in the heart and mind of the believer, harvested in the life, and shown to the world.

James is relevant. He's passionate. He's uncomplicated. He's direct.

James answers the question, "So what?"

And now, more than ever, its practical and principled message must be heard, heeded, and applied by twenty-first century Christians. This is the church's only hope for restoring its relevance as a confident voice of biblical morality and gospel truth.

It's the only way for a Christian to live.

January, 2012

*U*nder the Oak

I don't know how long it's been there, but I hope and expect it will outlive me—and my children and grandchildren, too.

When my wife, Beth, came to Texas nearly ten years ago in search of a home for us, she picked this one because of the special backyard. Nothing fancy, mind you. But there they stood, about thirty feet apart: two beautiful oaks. They were good-sized trees, strong and stately. For me, it was love at first sight. I've always had a deep respect and affection for trees, an appreciation handed down by my New England dad and my rural childhood.

Once, when I visited northern California and a friend took me to a state park, I stood among the Redwoods for the first time and felt like it was the closest I'd ever come to being in the Vatican. It was a truly awesome experience. I couldn't help but think of the brevity of man.

Several years ago, I decided to make the base of the further oak in my backyard a sanctuary. It didn't take much. I planted a lawn chair and next to it a small table. That's it. It's where I've gone to be with God, and just to rest and listen to the sounds of life.

On some mornings, even during the hottest days of summer, I've felt a gentle breeze flutter through the leaves that form my canopy. I have felt suddenly and strangely refreshed. I've looked up at the blue sky and known so keenly the sacred presence of God. Sometimes I've just sat there and wept tears of joy and gratitude for the abundant mercy and grace God has so undeservedly shown me.

I look forward to visiting with God there.

It's peaceful under that oak, and when I can sit there for a few moments and arrive at a place of peace in my own heart and mind, I can think about what matters most in this life. While the oak says nothing but just extends its branches over me, I think about heaven, eternity, death, blessings, and grace. I think about God. I think about Jesus. And when the next breeze blows, I also think about the wonderful mystery of the Holy Spirit.

Under that oak, I asked God to spare the life of my friend Michael when all hope was gone. And it was sitting under that tree that I listened by phone to my friend Chris give his life to Jesus.

Turmoil, division, fear, and anxiety are all around us. They assault our senses daily. Our economy is staggering and the world is reeling.

The times in which we live today were described by the Irish poet W.B. Yeats in his famous poem "The Second Coming:"

> *"Things fall apart; the centre cannot hold;*
> *Mere anarchy is loosed upon the world,*
> *The blood-dimmed tide is loosed, and everywhere*
> *The ceremony of innocence is drowned."*[39]

In the midst of these dangerous and difficult times, we speed to live our lives, struggle to meet expectations, and frantically fill our days. If it's not work, then it's amusement. While both work and pleasure are good and needful things, how many of us consistently take the time for solitude—for rest and peace and quietness?

We all need an oak tree in our lives.

We all need a time and a place to come apart from the "mere anarchy" and "blood-dimmed tide" that is everywhere loosed upon the earth.

> DO YOU HAVE A
> SPECIAL PLACE
> WHERE YOU GO
> TO BE ALONE
> WITH GOD?

Do you have a special place where you go to be alone with God?

You need that in your life. You and I need to experience the beauty and solitude of his peace. We will not find peace by looking to this world. This world is a churning cauldron of confusion: "things fall apart; the center cannot hold."

The prophet Isaiah wrote that God would keep us "in perfect peace" if our "thoughts are fixed" on him (Isaiah 26:3, NLT).

But to do that we must take the time to focus. And in order to focus on God, we must be alone and quiet with him. We seem sometimes to fear solitude, but solitude is a friend to lead us into the warm and welcoming presence of our heavenly Father.

He's waiting there for us.

Under the oak.

September, 2011

Chapter Nine: Dark Threads

"The dark threads were as needful
In the Weaver's skillful hand,
As the threads of gold and silver
In the pattern He had planned."

THE LOOM OF TIME, AUTHOR UNKNOWN

"Unearned suffering is redemptive."

MARTIN LUTHER KING JR.

*F*irst Sunday

I t fell on a Sunday.

The tenth anniversary of the most devastating attack upon America in our nation's history was marked on a day customarily reserved for widespread religious observance.

That's interesting.

We remember what happened during the morning hours of that clear blue Tuesday in September 2001. We recall where we were and what we were doing when we first heard the news. We remember the unimaginable television images broadcast around the world. We recall the shock and the grief; we remember the sadness and the mourning.

None of us can ever forget that day. While it seems difficult to imagine that more than an entire decade has gone by, for thousands of our fellow citizens who lost their dearest and best that September morning, the time has crawled by one lonely and heart-breaking day after another. They cope, they go on, and they remember. Like other defining events that helped to shape our nation, the well-planned terrorist attack upon the United States has been etched forever in collective American memory by its date alone. When we hear or read "9/11," we know instantly what it means. And we share a common reaction to the horror and the heroism that we all witnessed.

While the tragedy that day changed America and the world forever, how we feel about 9/11 will never change. In the weeks that followed, our country was united in a way that has happened only a few times in our history. We saw the noble spirit that is America rekindled; we saw a patriotism reborn. We saw rare courage and determination on display. We saw what it means to lead in crisis. We shared a national grief that broke our hearts—and brought us together. We also went back to church.

American statesman Adlai Stevenson once observed that "while we vote as many, we pray as one." In the days immediately following the attack, churches and synagogues—and yes, mosques too—filled to capacity. Our nation, as diverse as it is, looked up. We looked to an almighty and an all-loving God as together we sought comfort, strength, and courage in the midst of deep sadness and uncertainty. Americans instinctively knew, as did ancient Israel, that in crisis they needed help from a source greater than themselves. And so our nation turned to God for refuge, we turned to prayer for hope and solace.

"When the foundations crumble what can the righteous do?" (Psalm 11:3). It may seem a rhetorical question David posed. But in September 2001, many found an answer.

They went to church.

And in turning their hearts and minds to God, in entering the quietness and holiness of his sanctuary, they found the strength to face the future.

David did not let his question remain unanswered. He reaffirmed his belief in the sovereignty of God: "But the Lord is in his holy temple; the Lord still rules from heaven" (Psalm 11:4, NLT).

In the midst of national devastation, this is what we remembered. God is still in control. He will take us through—as individuals, as families, and as a nation. Our God reigns.

IN THE MIDST OF NATIONAL DEVASTATION, THIS IS WHAT WE REMEMBERED. GOD IS STILL IN CONTROL. HE WILL TAKE US THROUGH—AS INDIVIDUALS, AS FAMILIES, AND AS A NATION. OUR GOD REIGNS.

There is no attack he does not see, there is no crisis he cannot manage, there is no injustice he cannot avenge, and there is no heart he cannot comfort. "The Lord examines both the righteous and the wicked. He hates those who love violence… the righteous Lord loves justice. The virtuous will see his face" (Psalm 11: 5,7, NLT).

We did see his face—especially when we went to church. I will never forget that first Sunday after, at East Hampton Bible Church in Connecticut. Our small congregation was a genuine church family. We knew and loved one another. We were subdued with sadness but united by our concern and by our faith. There was an unusual stillness when I preached. God's people, worshiping a two-hour drive from the site of the attack, wanted to hear from God that morning a word of hope and comfort. They listened closely.

On the tenth anniversary of 9/11, I delivered the exact same message to Grace Heritage Community Church that I had preached ten years earlier. I made no changes. The words took us back to that time, back to the thoughts and feelings we had on that first Sunday.

"The Lord is in his holy temple; the Lord still rules from heaven."

September, 2011

ℳatt Chandler's Cancer

Here was a young pastor who seemed to have it all.

His vital and growing ministry had gained for him an expanding influence as he has led The Village Church in North Texas from 150 members to more than six thousand. He had a beautiful family and possessed the charisma, energy, and rare spiritual gifts that had made him a dynamic communicator of God's Word. His church loved him and followed him. Other pastors, especially young reformed theologians across the country, respected and listened to him.

At thirty-five, his future looked not only bright. It appeared limitless.

And then Matt Chandler was diagnosed with brain cancer. There was not one of us who didn't ask, "Why?"

Matt and his wife Lauren battled the disease with dignity, hope, and a full and active faith. Thousands around the world prayed for his recovery, believing in a God of might and miracles. Matt received the best medical care available and his church was a solid rock of encouragement and love. The media picked up on the story of Matt's crisis and that was wonderful because Matt was a heroic example of "suffering well."

But what does this mean, to "suffer well"?

It's an important question because while this happened to Matt Chandler, it could have happened to any of us. Suffering is a shared human lot and pain is a universal language. Peter refers to suffering fifteen times in his first letter and he uses eight different Greek words to express it. The Bible doesn't skirt pain—it confronts it head on.

The suffering of God's people in the first century—the trials and persecutions—is the stuff of legends. The church of Jesus Christ was born out of an inspiring mixture of joy and anguish, of pain and hope. No one can spend time reading the Bible without marveling at the great mystery and inescapable reality of suffering.

> PETER REFERS TO SUFFERING FIFTEEN TIMES IN HIS FIRST LETTER AND HE USES EIGHT DIFFERENT GREEK WORDS TO EXPRESS IT. THE BIBLE DOESN'T SKIRT PAIN—IT CONFRONTS IT HEAD ON.

Nothing focuses our attention and clarifies our priorities like pain. This is why C.S. Lewis called it "God's megaphone." In a message to his church during his battle, Matt Chandler wrestled with the idea of God's will and purpose in suffering. He spoke of the "tensions created in Scripture" and of his tenacious quest for answers and understanding. These were the transparent confessions of a sufferer who believed in the sovereignty of an omniscient God and hoped for his favor and healing.[40]

"We went to every doctor's appointment," Matt wrote, "only to have things go exactly opposite the way we had hoped and prayed." Matt said that he and Lauren "had to smile" at the reality of Proverbs 16:9: "We can make our plans, but the Lord determines our steps" (NLT).

Matt also described the theological tug-of-war among Christians, some of whom accept God as a kind of "uncaring, absentee landlord" whose omnipotence is viewed with a spirit of fatalism, and others who believe that with just a bit more prayer and faith, God—a sort of "genie who can be controlled"—will do whatever is asked. "Both camps reduce God to something He's not," Matt concluded.[41]

He wrote:

"My plan is to grow old, to walk my girls down the aisle, to see my boy grow up and marry a godly woman and become a godly man. I hope and pray for those things. My wife and I aggressively fight for those things, and we believe that's how it's going to play out. But if it doesn't, there's no bitterness in my heart."[42]

A man named Paul, who was no stranger to suffering and would give his life for the cause of Christ, told the Philippians:

"For I fully expect and hope that I will never be ashamed, but that I will continue to be bold for Christ, as I have been in the past. And I trust that my life will bring honor to Christ, whether I live or die" (Philippians 1:20, NLT).

That's a pretty good description of what it means to "suffer well."

May, 2010

"*M*ichael, Come Forth!"

He was dead, I was quite certain of it.

His wife, Cheryl, had called me earlier that morning to tell me that he had gone into the hospital. "When you see him, Jack, he won't be able to speak to you. He's on a ventilator."

I was unprepared for what I saw in that hospital room.

My precious friend Dr. Michael Tucker was stretched out on a bed, hooked up to more machinery than I had ever seen connected to a body. He was unconscious, his eyelids puffy and blue. His skin was cold. The only noise was the monotonous repetition of the machinery keeping him technically alive. The only difference was that he wasn't dressed up and lying in casket.

I spoke to him and I prayed for him.

I was stunned and broke down weeping. Cheryl, an RN, gently led me from the room. She calmly told me, "Michael is very sick." I couldn't grasp the suddenness of it. Three days earlier I had spoken on the phone with Mike about the visit he and his teenage son Michael had with former President Bush at a book signing at a Barnes & Noble. Mike was feeling fine. He and I had scheduled lunch for Friday. Ten days earlier he had been a guest lecturer in my government class and held forth for an hour on his assessment of the upcoming midterm elections.

Now he was dying.

The doctors didn't know the cause, but whatever virus had entered his body found a point of weakness and spread rapidly. It was tantamount to a system-wide failure. His one kidney was infected and losing strength. He had pneumonia in both lungs and he was septic. He was unable to breathe on his own and the doctors had induced a coma to try and save him. They were unable to even remove him from his room for a CAT scan, so precarious was his condition. When they finally could, the results showed that even if he should survive, he might have extensive brain damage.

After no improvement for two days, the doctors told Cheryl that short of a miracle, there was no hope.

When I told my wife Beth, her immediate response was: "Well, then we need to pray for a miracle."

"Well, we need to pray for God's will," I replied. "I mean, this is a pretty desperate situation. And I know Mike believes in the sovereignty of God."

"Yes," Beth answered, "but God would also have us pray for Mike's full recovery, even if that takes a miracle."

I knew she was right. Thank God for a woman of faith!

When his servants caught up with Jairus, who had just pleaded with Jesus to come and heal his daughter, they told him, "It's no use, your daughter is dead. Don't trouble the Teacher anymore."

But Jesus rebuffed the medical status quo: "Don't be afraid," he told them, "only believe, and she shall be made whole" (Luke 8:49, 50). When they all arrived at Jairus' home, those inside laughed at Jesus. In fact, the Bible says they "laughed him to scorn."

Luke says: "Because they all knew she was dead" (8:53).

Face the facts. Face reality. There is no hope. Not here. Not now.

But Jesus challenged the medical status quo again. He defied the power of death.

It seems that sometimes we want to believe in a miracle. We know a miracle is possible. But we fear truly praying for one. We don't want to get our hopes up. And we don't want to be disappointed with God. And so we resist the risk that faith pushes us to take.

After all, death is a powerful enemy.

That afternoon, I walked out to our backyard and sat in my chair underneath the oak tree. It's often where I go to meet with God. I slowly began to pray for Mike. I wept. Then I prayed some more, but then I wept again. Finally, I remembered that Jesus prayed at the tomb of Lazarus. He thanked his Father for hearing him. He prayed that those standing there, watching and waiting, might believe.

And then he cried with a loud voice: "Lazarus, come forth!"

And he did.

I asked God to heal Mike. "For your glory, that those watching might know that you are truly God, I beg you to heal Mike." I know that many joined me in that prayer.

> GOD DOESN'T HEAL EVERYONE, BUT WE MUST NEVER FORGET THAT HE CAN. AND WE SHOULD NEVER BE AFRAID TO ASK HIM.

A few days later, Beth and I visited Mike and Cheryl and their son David at the hospital. Mike was sitting in a chair next to his bed. He wasn't hooked up to a thing! He laughed, we talked politics. He wanted to be home soon.

"That's my goal," Mike smiled. I knew he was back.

And before we left, we all held hands and thanked God for his mighty miracle.

God doesn't heal everyone, but we must never forget that he can. And we should never be afraid to ask him.

"Don't be afraid. Only believe."

January, 2011

_Tears in a Bottle

N ow who am I going to talk to?"
     Keely Vanacker asked that question in November 2009.

Keely's father, Michael Grant Cahill, along with twelve other men and women, was a victim of the tragedy that occurred at the Fort Hood Army base. Another seemingly random act of violence that left us stunned, wondering how and why. Keely Vanacker remembered those long talks with her dad after Thanksgiving dinners.

The victims ranged in age from nineteen to sixty-two. Their backgrounds and personalities, and what led them to Fort Hood, varied greatly, but their sudden deaths united them. This national tragedy also united their families in a grief both unexpected and unexplained. When our lives are suddenly turned upside down by shock and heartbreak, there is no time to prepare ourselves emotionally. We are plunged into the icy deep waters of grief. This is especially so when it is the result not of an accident, but of the intentional violence of another.

Offering comfort in a loss so overwhelming is no easy thing.

Christians are, unfortunately, not always adept at giving comfort. How do we respond? What do we say? How do we explain? And why do we feel the need to? Why is it that we so often feel compelled to have an answer when pain and suffering strike? Perhaps it is because we are nervous about the age-old incongruity of suffering and God's compassion. We know that many are asking the same question: "Why?" And so we are tempted to resort to Scripture, and theology, and all manner of analysis. It's our own awkward way of comforting. And besides, God needs defending in this situation.

Doesn't he?

We talk because we fear the silence.

Yet, when people in grief need support more than protection, a silent presence may be the best comfort of all. There are no pat answers. It is only cruelty to suggest otherwise. And God's will? What comfort is there in speculating to those who hurt about a divinity that in times of suffering is intentionally shrouded in mystery?

We stand and rely on what we know: God is love. And because he is, his heart breaks with ours. He weeps with us, as Jesus wept at the grave of his friend. God's purpose in tragedy may be concealed, but his compassion and kindness are not. Unlike the Greek gods who made sport with the fates of mortals, the true God gathers us in his arms of love.

> GOD'S PURPOSE IN TRAGEDY MAY BE CONCEALED, BUT HIS COMPASSION AND KINDNESS ARE NOT.

When his son Alex died in an automobile accident at the age of twenty-four, Rev. William Sloan Coffin told his parishioners in a sermon at the famed Riverside Church in New York City that "my own consolation lies in knowing... that when the waves closed in over the sinking car, God's heart was the first of all our hearts to break."[43]

The psalmist speaks over and over again of the comfort, compassion, and remembrance of God; of his tenderness toward those who sorrow. God's tenderness is our strength. And it is our final and best source of comfort.

David writes in the fifty-sixth Psalm:

"You keep track of all my sorrows. You have collected all my tears in your bottle. You have recorded each one in your book" (Psalm 56:8, NLT). It's a beautiful metaphor that expresses the intimacy of God's concern when we hurt. God keeps track of us. He maintains a full record. He misses nothing. He knows the details of our heartache that no one else knows. He writes down each one.

You think no one understands? God understands.

God not only knows. God cares. God weeps. He traces our grief with his love. He keeps all our tears in his bottle. And he's written each one in his book.

November, 2009

When Children Die

"Parents are not supposed to bury their children."

We've all heard that. We've all thought it. It's what we all believe.

But we all know it's not what happens.

Children die.

I recently conducted the funeral of a twenty-one-year-old man killed in a motorcycle accident. Then, near Liberty Christian School, a twelve-year-old boy—an outgoing and fun-loving sixth grader there—was killed in a freakish traffic accident.

Shock is always the default reaction. What's happened is unnatural: sudden, devastating, and inexplicable. After the shock comes what I call the "Perplexities of Providence," best summarized in this straightforward rhetorical question:

"Why would an all-powerful and all-loving God permit such a thing to happen?"

Theologians and ministers attempt to answer that question. We are seldom successful.

To live by faith is to reject the premise and implications of a life lived only by sight. Christianity is based on the idea of a greater and keener reality beyond the senses and beyond the present. One may not think it relevant to draw upon Christian doctrine to comfort the family of a child who has died. Yet in fact, it is the ultimate comfort.

Truth—not mere sentiment or sympathy—is the only thing that can stand up to grief. Jesus told us this in a story about the man who had built his house upon the rock instead of the sand. When the storms of life came—as they always do—his house remained.

Our hope must be built upon a firm theological foundation or it will offer to us neither hope nor comfort when the storms hit. This is why sound doctrine is so vital to our lives.

Christian author Philip Yancey argued that the resurrection of Jesus Christ proved that this world is the illusion and that heaven is the reality.[44] In his letter to the Romans, Paul wrote powerfully of the sad and weary captivity of this fallen and corrupted world. It is a world where sin and Satan work to destroy all hope. This is a world in which children die.

Paul acknowledged that we suffer—that pain and loss can nearly overwhelm us—but he pointed us to a "future glory" and liberation as our ultimate hope. He told us to wait "patiently and confidently" for this coming day. And Paul placed our hope in a broader perspective. "For all of creation is waiting eagerly for that future day... when it will join God's children in glorious freedom from death and decay" (Romans 8:19-21, NLT).

The world says, "Time is a great healer. You'll see, things will get better." The Bible tells us, "This shall not stand!"

THIS IS TRUTH. THIS IS DOCTRINE. THIS IS OUR FAITH. THIS IS OUR SECURITY. THIS IS OUR COMFORT. THIS IS OUR STRENGTH.

As Jesus prepared to go through his own agony on the cross, he told his disciples, "In this world [the one held captive by sin] you will have many trials and sorrows." (John 16:33, NLT). In this world people will get cancer. People will die in natural disasters. They will suffer from disease and poverty. There will be injustice and exploitation.

In this world, children will die.

Then Jesus tells us this: "But take heart, because I have overcome the world" (John 16:33, NLT).

How has Jesus "overcome the world"? He defeated death and the devil when he rose again. He secured for us that "future glory." He invites us to live by faith in the continuing and confident hope of the final victory he has already won. We weep now in the night of our captivity. But the joy of a new day is coming. And then "there will be no more death or sorrow or crying or pain. All these things are gone forever" (Revelation 21: 4, NLT). This is truth. This is doctrine. This is our faith. This is our security. This is our comfort. This is our strength.

And this is our hope, even when children die.

January, 2010

$\mathscr{G}$ood Stuff

L ittle Tony was a slow learner in school.

He was taunted constantly. His classmates called him "Dumbo." His grandfather told Tony's mother, "Tony's got a big head; pity there's nothing in it." Tony's teachers all agreed: he wouldn't amount to much. He was brought before the school headmaster, who told the young man there was something wrong with him. One teacher twisted his ear until it broke because Tony couldn't understand arithmetic. "You are only fit to grease your father's bread tins," the abusive teacher told him.

Tony's dad came to his defense and threatened the teacher if he ever laid a hand on Tony again. Then his dad told him: "You've got to toughen up. Learn to stand up for yourself." So Tony resolved then and there to make his trials steppingstones to strength.

And he did.

Years later, in looking back on the difficulties and struggles of his youth, Tony remarked, "It's not 'poor me' at all. It was all good stuff."[45]

What goes through the heart and mind of a child who is told he will be a failure? For Tony, adversity ended up an ally. Criticism and abuse stiffened his determination to succeed. That's not always the case, but for him it was.

There's not a person reading this who hasn't faced some form of crisis.

There's not one of us who hasn't been tested. We have all gone through our own personal valley of despair; we all have experienced heartache, disappointment, defeat. Facing struggles is part of life in this world. Few escape being tested in some way.

Job plainly confessed that suffering is a lonely path. He looked for God in the midst of his despair. Job looked north, south, east, and west "but I cannot find him. I do not see him... for he is hidden... he is concealed" (Job 23:8, 9, NLT). But Job decided to place his faith in the invisible but still present God. "And when he tests me [in the white-hot fires of affliction] I will come out as pure gold" (Job 23:10, NLT).

If the Bible teaches anything, it teaches that suffering—hardships, injustice, abuse, sickness, pain—is redemptive. Adversity is not to be escaped but endured as a vital part of what makes us stronger and better and deeper. Without it, we can never become mature in Christ.

> ADVERSITY IS NOT TO BE ESCAPED BUT ENDURED AS A VITAL PART OF WHAT MAKES US STRONGER AND BETTER AND DEEPER. WITHOUT IT, WE CAN NEVER BECOME MATURE IN CHRIST.

The apostle Paul, who had considerable firsthand experience with this sort of thing, told the Romans to "rejoice" when trials and problems come. "For we know that they help us develop endurance. And endurance develops strength of character, and character strengthens our confident hope of salvation. And this hope will not lead to disappointment."

Why?

"For we know how dearly God loves us" (Romans 5:3-5, NLT).

So who is Tony, the man who determined to overcome his childhood? Sir Anthony Hopkins, one of the greatest and most accomplished actors of our time.

And like him, hopefully we'll be able to look back on the trials and hardships God sends into our own lives and say, "It was all good stuff."

April, 2010

Chapter Ten: The Crucible

"Without courage all other virtues lose their meaning."
WINSTON CHURCHILL

$\mathscr{K}$eep the Gate Shut

I love dogs.

That's just part of the baggage that comes with being me. I grew up with them. My dad hunted rabbits with beagles, then later raccoons with other hounds. I just find dogs fascinating, fun, affectionate, and very loyal.

And then there's Jesse.

Our daughter's Rhodesian Ridgeback is staying with us until she and her husband get a place of their own where they can have him. That doesn't include their present third-story apartment. So we've got Jesse. He's OK. But I've always thought him a bit strange. While our own dog, Maggie, an eleven-year-old lab, knows enough to stay home, Jesse likes to wander the neighborhood. We've had some close calls with Highland Village's zealous law enforcement, so we have to be extra careful.

Jesse is harmless enough. He's not intending to do anything wrong. It's just that he's curious. So we have to keep an eye on him. Jesse needs boundaries.

That's why my wife often reminds me, "Keep the gate shut." If we don't, Jesse could wander. He could get into trouble.

I don't know what time of year it was when King David was doing some wandering of his own. I'm betting it might have been a beautiful summer evening. And there was Bathsheba: "splash, splash, taking a bath." The rest, as they say, is history. The king, a bit bored in his palace while his army fought, wandered. David got into trouble. A lot of trouble, it turned out.

David didn't shut the gate.

"Why are you so angry," the Lord asked Cain, who was in what police call "a jealous rage" over his brother's better sacrifice. "You will be accepted," God told him, "if you do what is right." Then God gave Cain a somber warning that has rung tragically true down through the corridors of time, like a bell in the night. "But if you refuse to do what is right, then watch out! Sin is crouching at the door, eager to control you. But you must subdue it and be its master" (Genesis 4:6, 7, NLT).

Sin was hiding just outside the gate—the gate that Cain didn't shut.

James was pretty blunt about a lot of things in his New Testament letter. One of those topics was temptation. Don't blame God for that, James writes. God "never tempts anyone. Temptation comes from our own desires, which entice us and drag us away. These desires give birth to sinful actions. And when sin is allowed to grow, it gives birth to death" (James 1: 13-15, NLT).

TEMPTATION IS A PROCESS, NEVER A SINGLE IMPULSIVE ACT.

Temptation is a process, never a single impulsive act. Eve saw the forbidden fruit before she ever tasted it.

Our popular culture screams at the top of its lungs, "Go ahead, it's OK! Look, isn't that cool (or is the better word "hot"?)? There's nothing wrong with just a peek, just a taste, just a brief moment." Television, and especially the omnipresent Internet, invite us into a virtual "Vanity Fair" of sinful pleasures. Who's going to know? And it all begins with the curiosity of our eyes.

Like Jesse, we like to wander.

"Opportunity knocks but once," observed Mark Twain. "Temptation leans on the door bell."

So keep the gate shut.

August, 2010

"*B*ut If Not..."

The Crucible: Part One

I t was a desperate and apparently hopeless situation.
There was no way out.

In one of the most famous military episodes of World War II, along the coast of France, at a place called Dunkirk, Allied forces were facing a staggering defeat by the invading German army. There seemed to be no escape.

In an article in *Vanity Fair* magazine, Christopher Hitchens recounted how a British officer, stranded on the beach with his soldiers in that spring of 1940, sent a simple cable back home. The message contained three words: "But if not..."

Hitchens said of the officer's message, "All those who received it were at once aware of what it signified." And then Hitchens referred to one of the most famous stories found in the Bible. We read about it in the third chapter of the book of Daniel.[46]

After King Nebuchadnezzar had a ninety-foot gold statue made, he ordered everyone in his kingdom—"whatever their race, or nation or language"—to bow before it and worship it. Compliance was helped immeasurably by the threat of a human barbecue in a fiery furnace for anyone who didn't obey. The story says that "all the people" complied with the order.

Everybody, that is, except three young Jews. They ignored the king's command.

Brought before the king, Shadrach, Meshach, and Abednego were given one final chance to bow down and worship the golden statue.

But the three young men kept their cool. We don't know who spoke for this brave trio, but here's what one of them told the king in reply:

"O Nebuchadnezzar, we are not careful to answer thee in this matter."

No hesitancy, no equivocation, no fear, and no doubt: just a calm assurance—and a bold confidence.

"If it be so, our God whom we serve is able to deliver us from the burning fiery furnace, and he will deliver us out of thine hand, O king" (Daniel 3:16, 17, KJV).

Here is quiet strength, enormous courage, and incredible faith in the midst of a literal life-and-death crisis. It's one of the greatest declarations of trust in God you'll find anywhere in the Bible.

Except for the next one.

"But if not, be it known unto thee, O king, that we will not serve thy gods, nor worship the golden image which thou hast set up" (Daniel 3:18, KJV).

"But if not…"

With this, these three lads stepped up squarely to the plate of faith.

It is one thing for us to have faith in God because we believe it will lead to a positive outcome.

It's quite another for us to place our faith—and our very lives—in the mighty hands of a sovereign God, whatever the outcome.

The greatest faith is when you and I trust God—and decide to honor and obey him—whatever the cost, whatever the sacrifice, and whatever the result. Genuine Christian faith is not a manipulation. It is an abandonment. Real trust in God is not based on our expected deliverance. It is rooted in God's perfect will.

> WE HONOR GOD NOT "IN ORDER THAT." WE TRUST GOD "EVEN IF."

We honor God not "in order that." We trust God "even if."

We know what happened to the three young Hebrews. We just don't know what was going through their minds as they were being bound and lifted up for the final cookout.

Any last-second thoughts?

"But if not…"

Dunkirk? Adolph Hitler, for some strange and inexplicable reason, halted the German march for three days. Enough time for 338,000 allied troops to escape.

It's another reminder of the courage of our soldiers—and the amazing providence of God.

May, 2011

The Fourth Man
The Crucible: Part Two

They were in a hot spot.

These three Jewish kids had defied the law of the land. They had been arrested and brought before the king.

There are usually consequences for breaking the law—even an unjust one. When Henry David Thoreau was locked up for refusing to pay his taxes because he opposed the Mexican War, his friend Ralph Waldo Emerson visited him in jail. "Why Henry, what are you doing in here?" Emerson asked. To which Thoreau immediately replied: "Ralph, what are you doing out there?"

Civil disobedience: Thoreau wrote a book about it.

Shadrach, Meshach, and Abednego practiced it. They had defied King Nebuchadnezzar's edict to bow down when the music played and refused to worship the ninety-foot golden statue the king had built. But the penalty for this civil disobedience—this declaration of religious conscience—wasn't thirty days in the county slammer. These guys were being thrown headlong into a giant blazing furnace, to be burned alive. The old king got so hot under the collar because of their bold impudence that he ordered the furnace heated "seven times hotter than usual" (Daniel 3:19, NLT).

At this point, one might wonder what these young men were thinking. "Not a long life, perhaps, but a life lived well." "No compromise." "May God be merciful and not let us suffer." "If this is the end, then let it be swift." But where was the God they had served and obeyed? Where was the God for whom they were prepared to die?

Was God going to just stand by and let these young men perish?

Where is he? Ever ask that question?

It is a great irony of our faith that often when we feel we need him most, God seems the most distant. In the very midst of our crisis, our prayers seem the least effective. We sense, in our lonely vigil of heartache, that God is removed and aloof from our suffering and pain. Perhaps part of the answer is that we feel our trial is something that God could have prevented but didn't. So there is a disappointment with God—that somehow he failed us. That perhaps he doesn't love us as much as we had hoped, or maybe he doesn't care.

In *A Grief Observed*, written after his wife died of cancer, C.S. Lewis said: *"Meanwhile, where is God? When you are happy... if you turn to Him then with praise, you will be welcomed with open arms. But go to Him when your need is desperate, when all other help is vain and what do you find? A door slammed in your face, and a sound of bolting and double bolting on the inside. After that, silence. You may as well turn away."*[47]

> WITH GOD, THE REALITY MUST ALWAYS TRUMP THE IMPRESSION, EVEN FOR SO GREAT A MAN AS LEWIS. GOD DOES HIS FINEST WORK IN US—AND FOR US—THROUGH OUR AFFLICTIONS: THROUGH OUR PAIN AND OUR GRIEF.

Anyone who's ever suffered can identify with that.

But with God, the reality must always trump the impression, even for so great a man as Lewis. God does his finest work in us—and for us—through our afflictions: through our pain and our grief.

The Lord tells Israel: "I have refined you, but not as silver is refined. Rather, I have refined you in the furnace of suffering" (Isaiah 48:10, NLT).

"But suddenly, Nebuchadnezzar jumped up in amazement and exclaimed to his advisers, 'Didn't we tie up three men and throw them into the furnace?

"'Yes, Your Majesty, we certainly did.'

"'Look!' Nebuchadnezzar shouted. 'I see four men, unbound, walking around in the fire unharmed! And the fourth looks like a god'" (Daniel 3:24, 25, NLT).

The King James Version says: "And the form of the fourth is like the Son of God."

The God who was with the young Hebrews in their moment of crisis is the same God who is with us. The Savior who rescued Shadrach, Meshach, and Abednego is the same Jesus who will rescue you out of your furnace of suffering.

He's the fourth man. In your crisis—in your pain and heartache; in your doubt, fear, and uncertainty—where is God?

He's still in the fire.

June, 2011

$\mathscr{A}$ Time for Choosing

The Crucible: Part Three

He had been warned: his career would be ruined. His life had even been threatened. There was enormous pressure to conform to the expectations.

In the end, it all came down to one decision—one choice. It would be the most important one of his career. And it would also be one of the most important choices in American history. When U.S. Senator Edmund G. Ross of Kansas was called to choose, he voted to acquit President Andrew Johnson. The president had been impeached for "high crimes and misdemeanors."

As the seventh of seven Republican senators to break with his party and vote to acquit Johnson, Ross cast the deciding vote to save the embattled president. Johnson finished his term. Ross, however, lost his seat in the Senate two years later. His career in elective office was over. Years later, after history had judged Johnson's impeachment to have been a matter of vengeful politics, Ross was included as a chapter in John Kennedy's book *Profiles in Courage*.

Ross was vindicated, but he had paid a price for his courageous stand. It was a choice of yes or no–convict or acquit. There was no "straddle" option. No third choice. No "perhaps." It was a straight up and down vote. And the stakes were high.

The poet James Russell Lowell wrote:

"Once to every man and nation, comes the moment to decide,
In the strife of truth with falsehood, for the good or evil side;
Some great cause, some great decision, offering each the bloom or
blight,
And the choice goes by forever, 'twixt that darkness and that light."[48]

Because that choice is never easy, many will do their best to avoid it.

For the Christian—especially one in leadership—the avenues of escape are gradually narrowing. As our American culture crumbles and the church flirts ever more audaciously with apostasy, the true follower of Jesus Christ must choose.

We must choose between the world and the Word; between compromise and conviction; between popularity and principle. Eventually the choice we postpone will be forced upon us.

Tolerance and pluralism are all the rage—the sophisticated hallmarks of our postmodern era. But the Christian would do well to remember the wise observation of G.K. Chesterton: "Tolerance is the virtue of a man without convictions."

As churches pursue growth, temptations mount. Will we seek an audience to hear the message of truth, or will we temper and tailor the message to win an audience?

> WE MUST CHOOSE BETWEEN THE WORLD AND THE WORD; BETWEEN COMPROMISE AND CONVICTION; BETWEEN POPULARITY AND PRINCIPLE. EVENTUALLY THE CHOICE WE POSTPONE WILL BE FORCED UPON US.

Evangelical warhorses like John Piper and John MacArthur flared their nostrils at Rob Bell's *Love Wins* heresy about hell. For younger evangelical leaders, with one eye on the twenty-something crowd, it was more like the sin that dare not speak its name. The high-profiles were suddenly low on courage.

There will doubtless be other major theological fault lines in the years ahead.

When forced to choose, what choice will we make?

Shadrach, Meshach, and Abednego could easily have folded. They could have—just once—given a little nod to the idols of their age and the order of their king. Who would have blamed them? Everyone else was doing it. And the stakes—their lives—couldn't have been any higher.

For the young Hebrews, it was a time for choosing. They chose.

Daniel could have chosen to keep his prayers hidden and silent rather than risk being the main course for some hungry lions. For him, it was a time for choosing. Daniel chose.

The writer of Hebrews tells us that Moses, in the prime of his promising life, "chose to share the oppression of God's people instead of enjoying the fleeting pleasures of sin. He thought it was better to suffer for the sake of Christ than to own the treasures of Egypt..." (Hebrews 11:25, 26, NLT).

These patriarchs are among the silent "cloud of witnesses" that watch, wait, and pray–for you and for me, and the choices we make.

"Choose today whom you will serve" (Joshua 24:16).

June, 2011

The Look

We all mess up.

We fail. We sin. We miss the mark—by a lot or a little makes no difference. The glory of God is a very high standard and there's not one mortal who hasn't fallen short of it.

Yet no failure must ever be final.

No sin must ever be fatal.

A man called Peter could tell us.

It would have been bad enough that evening for him. But Peter typically was the one who spoke up, and that only made it worse. Jesus had just warned him: "Simon, Simon, Satan has asked to sift each of you like wheat. I have pleaded in prayer for you, Simon, that your faith should not fail. So when you have repented and turned to me again, strengthen your brothers" (Luke 22:31, 32, NLT).

You might expect Peter to have cautiously pondered that spiritual advisory, coming as it did from his Lord. But then, he was Peter, after all.

"Lord," he insisted, "I am ready to go to prison with you, and even die with you" (Luke 22:33, NLT).

All of us pledge enthusiastic loyalty at the outset—and we're always sincere in the moment. Devotion comes easy until it's put to the test. Courage means nothing until it's called for. We're always ready to march—before we actually have to. So, at the time he spoke those words, Peter meant them.

What Jesus then told Peter—perhaps in the presence of the other disciples—stunned him to silence. "Peter, let me tell you something. Before the rooster crows tomorrow morning, you will deny three times that you even know me" (22:34, NLT).

> ALL OF US PLEDGE ENTHUSIASTIC LOYALTY AT THE OUTSET—AND WE'RE ALWAYS SINCERE IN THE MOMENT.

And so it was, as the dark evening wore on, that Peter's loyalty began to unravel and the courage he had so passionately professed evaporated into the night mist. First, he couldn't even stay awake through Jesus' agony in the Garden of Gethsemane. While Jesus wept, Peter slept. As his Lord—the one for whom Peter would be willing to die—was led away by the Temple guards, "Peter followed *at a distance*" (Luke 22:54, emphasis added, NLT).

And then came the expletive-laced denials.

Jesus had renamed him "Peter"—the Rock. But now he had crumbled like soapstone.

Luke tells us something that the other gospel writers omit. After Peter said—for the third time—that he didn't know who Jesus was, Luke records:

"At that moment the Lord turned and looked at Peter" (22:61, NLT).

I don't know how Luke could have known that startling detail—except that Peter must have told him. Peter must have remembered that look of his Lord. How could he ever forget those eyes, so sad yet so very kind? Was it not a look of understanding and compassion? Surely, Jesus didn't scowl at Peter. It could not have been a look of condemnation or anger. It was, I believe, a brief look of tender heartbrokenness.

However Jesus looked at Peter in that instant, the impact was immediate. "Suddenly, the Lord's words flashed through Peter's mind" (22:61, NLT). "And Peter remembered the word of the Lord." (KJV).

Luke says that "Peter left the courtyard, weeping bitterly" (22:62, NLT).

Peter disappears into his shame and disgrace and his incredible guilt. Yes, "Peter remembered" alright. That's all he could do. He remembered the courage he had when it didn't matter. And the courage he lost when it did. He remembered how his lofty loyalty disintegrated under stress.

Most of all, Peter recalled the look.

How could Jesus ever forgive him? How could Jesus ever look at Peter—again? But Luke tells us that the buzz following the resurrection was that "the Lord has really risen!" How did they know?

"He has appeared to Peter" (Luke 24:34, NLT). Yes, Peter!

Mark says that the young man at Jesus' empty tomb had commanded the women who had come to anoint Jesus' body to "go, tell his disciples and Peter" that Jesus had risen (Mark 16:7, NASB).

"...and Peter..." Don't forget Peter.

Peter, whose greatest days were still ahead. Peter, who would strengthen, encourage, and lead the first Christian church. Peter, would yet die for Christ. Yes, Peter, who was forgiven and still loved by the savior he had denied knowing.

It has been said that "we need to be loved the most when we deserve it the least. Only God can fulfill this need. Only God can provide a love so deep it saves from the depths."

Peter could tell us that. He saw The Look.

March, 2012

The Shadow Knows

One of the most popular radio programs in the 1930s was called *The Shadow*. It centered on a mysterious crime-fighter with psychic powers, named Lamont Cranston, aka The Shadow. Even decades later, the program's famous introduction could still be repeated by many:

"Who knows what evil lurks in the hearts of men? The Shadow knows!" This was followed by a sinister laugh. The tagline was made even more memorable when the voice was Orson Welles.

At the end of the second chapter of John's gospel, we find an interesting, often overlooked passage. John says that "because of the miraculous signs Jesus did in Jerusalem at the Passover celebration, many began to trust in him" (John 2:23, NLT). One might think that Jesus would have welcomed such professions of faith and been pleased with the effectiveness of his ministry. Instead, one is caught off guard by his reaction:

"But Jesus didn't trust them, because he knew human nature. No one needed to tell him what mankind is really like" (vs. 24, 25, NLT).

Jesus understood the human condition. He knew the human heart. He knew what was there and he knew what it meant for civilization. The one who delivered the Sermon on the Mount also knew how hard it would be to put it into practice.

Jesus knew that in this very city of Jerusalem, the day would come when adoring crowds wanting to make him king would turn on him and demand his death. He knew his closest and most loyal followers, those men into whom Jesus had poured his life for three years, would forsake him when he needed them most. They would run and hide.

Jesus was nothing if not realistic about human nature.

You and I are morally and spiritually incorrigible. No amount of sunny side up motivational pep talks can change that. We're a mess. The first step to knowing ourselves for who we truly are is to acknowledge this central truth—you and I are lost. More lost than those TV characters stranded on that island. Our nature is fundamentally warped; it is deformed by a sickness called sin.

Here's the good news: God's grace is richer, fuller, and far deeper than the depth of our total depravity. His grace can save us, change us, and give us hope for a better life, both now and in the future. Jesus knew the nature of the human heart. That's why he came. Jesus knew what evil could lurk there, and that's why he died. Christ came, he died, and he rose again so that we could be re-created—given a new heart.

By God's amazing grace, we are not simply reformed on the outside, in our manners, appearance, and our virtues. We are transformed on the inside, in our spirit, our attitude, and our reason for living. We call this regeneration. We call this being born again.

It's a good thing Christ knew man for what he truly is by his nature, evil to the core. For only then could Jesus provide the remedy to make man what he could truly be, a child of God. The psalmist is comforting when he tells us that "God knows how weak we are; he remembers we are only dust" (Psalm 103:14, NLT). This divine appreciation is very reassuring.

> REDEMPTION AND TRANSFORMATION BEGIN WITH RECOGNITION. THEY BEGIN WITH THE PLAIN TRUTH OF WHO—AND WHAT—WE ARE.

Redemption and transformation begin with recognition. They begin with the plain truth of who—and what—we are. For only then do we realize that we cannot possibly save ourselves. Only then do we admit that this world cannot perfect itself. Only then do we know we are doomed without a redeemer.

"Who knows what evil lurks in the hearts of men? The Shadow knows."

So does the Savior.

June, 2010

When Joe Said No
Part One

Nobody would have blamed him.

He was young and handsome—and single. Today, he'd be called "hot."

She was rich, powerful, and lovely. She was the boss's wife but she really wanted Joe—badly.

We've seen this scenario many times before—played out in a thousand soap operas and Hollywood movies. Today, it's typical. It probably always has been.

The story of young Joseph's sexual temptation is recorded in Genesis 39. An Egyptian officer named Potiphar purchased the Hebrew slave and put him in charge of his household. Potiphar was captain of the guard for Pharaoh, the king of Egypt. Things went very well for Joseph—and things went great for Potiphar too, since God was going to bless the Egyptian ruler "for Joseph's sake" (Genesis 39:5).

Potiphar's wife attempted to lure Joseph into bed several times. But although "she kept putting pressure on Joseph day after day... he refused to sleep with her and he kept out of her way as much as possible" (Genesis 39:10, NLT).

"Opportunity knocks but once," said Mark Twain. "Temptation leans on the doorbell."

Joseph seemed to be a rock of resistance, but we all know that even a rock can sometimes crack. The Bible is filled with stories of the insidious triumph of temptation, beginning with Adam and Eve and going forward. And nowhere is this weapon of temptation more subtly and successfully wielded than in the treacherous waters of human sexuality.

High-profile episodes of infidelity have become so notoriously frequent that *Time* magazine ran a cover story on why powerful men have such a difficult time behaving themselves. There's usually a good woman behind every man's success—and often another one (or perhaps several)—behind his downfall.

There are plenty of ministers and politicians who could say "Amen" to that. What's interesting about the final confrontation in Joseph's gallant resistance is that it takes place when "no one else was around" (Genesis 39:11, NLT).

No one was watching but God.

It's not always easy to do right thing, to make the right choice. The most difficult time to maintain one's integrity is when sin looks very good, very easy, and very harmless. And the easiest time to fall is when there are no witnesses.

Joseph stood his ground. It was a remarkable feat for a healthy and "normal" young man.

And while by this time Potiphar's wife was plotting against him, and Joseph had no time to respond as she tore his coat, his earlier answer stirs inspiration for its fidelity in the face of betrayal.

Reminding her that her own husband had given him his full trust, Joseph told her: "How could I do such a wicked thing? It would be a great sin against God" (Genesis 39:9, NLT). Joseph could have viewed this as an act of human betrayal. That would be serious enough. His boss had been very good to him. But this young man appealed to an even higher loyalty.

Beloved Nazarene preacher and scholar W.T. Purkiser once wrote: "Temptation wins its easiest victories over those whose hearts are restless

> WHEN TEMPTATION DREW ITS LINE IN THE SANDS OF EGYPT, WHEN ALL THAT WAS NATURAL CRIED OUT FOR PLEASURE AT THE PRICE OF PRINCIPLE, JOSEPH SIDED WITH GOD.

and dissatisfied because the issue of their ultimate loyalty has never been fully settled."

For Joseph, the matter of his ultimate allegiance had been settled, though he was but a youth.

When temptation drew its line in the sands of Egypt, when all that was natural cried out for pleasure at the price of principle, Joseph sided with God.

May God give us the grace, courage, and the strength to do no less.

July, 2011

When Joe Said No
Part Two

L ife isn't always fair.

Even when God's in it.

You'd want to think that whenever we do the brave and right thing—when wrong is resisted and the good is affirmed—a loving God would immediately bless our faithfulness. But that's not what happened to Joseph when he chose to honor God instead of sinning with Potiphar's wife.

Making the morally right choice cost Joseph dearly. We might expect God to reward this young man for his integrity and moral courage. But he doesn't—not yet. Instead, God permits him to suffer an unjust punishment. When Potiphar's vengeful wife accuses Joseph of attempted rape, he is thrown in prison.

Joseph is falsely accused of doing wrong only because he insisted on doing right. And he pays a price, as true followers of a righteous God often do.

Yet God never forsakes the young Hebrew, but uses his false imprisonment to prepare Joseph for his moment of national greatness. Most of us know the rest of the story of this famed dreamer. Even in prison, God blesses him. And eventually, Joseph is "back in the high life again."

From betrayal by his brothers, through slavery and prison, to a position of power in Egypt second only to the Pharaoh, Joseph's life is a testament to the providence of our sovereign God. Several times in Genesis 39—as Joseph goes through the darkest valley of his life—we read that "the Lord was with him." My favorite verse in this entire chapter is verse 21:

"But the Lord was with Joseph in the prison and showed him his faithful love" (NLT).

Through our darkest, loneliest, and most heartbreaking nights, God is with us. When we are misunderstood, and criticized unfairly; when our "good is evil spoken of," God is with us. When we suffer for doing what is right, God is with us then, too. In every dark prison cell of our lives, God is with us. He shows his faithful love "through it all."

> THROUGH OUR DARKEST, LONELIEST, AND MOST HEARTBREAKING NIGHTS, GOD IS WITH US. HE SHOWS HIS FAITHFUL LOVE "THROUGH IT ALL."

No, life isn't always fair. But God is always present. He is always able and his plan is always perfect. You may not think he's there with you. You may neither see him nor feel him. You may even think God's left you there alone, forgotten you. If we're honest about it, many of us have felt, at some time in our lives, abandoned by God.

Joseph remained in prison for "some time" (Genesis 40:1, NLT). But God had not forgotten him. And God will never forget you. Isaiah the prophet offers us some good advice while we suffer and wait and while we wonder:

"If you are walking in darkness, without a ray of light, trust in the Lord and rely on your God" (Isaiah 50:10, NLT).

Because God is there in your darkness.

There is not one shred of bitterness or anger or resentment or grievance anywhere recounted in the remarkable life of Joseph. Not once do we read that he ever complained to God for all he went through. Even while he languished in prison, an innocent man condemned for doing the right thing. Joseph shames me in my own petty complaints and perceived injustices.

Years later, when he reconciled with the jealous brothers who had sold him into slavery, Joseph tenderly reassured them even as he confirmed his own faith in a faithful God: "You intended to harm me, but God intended it all for good. He brought me to this position so I could save the lives of many people" (Genesis 50:20, NLT).

Joseph had bravely said no to sin. And there came a time when God rewarded Joseph with his glorious yes!

If we'll honor him even in the darkest, most difficult times, God will not only bless us—he'll open our prison door and set us free.

August, 2011

When Courage Calls

In Shakespeare's play *Julius Caesar*, Mark Antony famously observed, "The evil men do lives after them; the good is oft interred with their bones."

As I read the many fine tributes paid to legendary football coach Joe Paterno upon his death in January 2012—and witnessed the national outpouring of grief and sadness at his passing—I could only hope that in this case Shakespeare would be proven wrong.

Paterno's record as head football coach at Penn State was amazing: a forty-six-year career that included two national championships, five unbeaten seasons, victories in all five major bowl games, and a place in the football Hall of Fame.

Joe Paterno was the most triumphant Division I coach in football history.

Which made the tragic end of his astonishing career all the sadder.

One of those who released a statement of praise and condolence to the media upon learning of Paterno's death was former coach Jerry Sandusky, Paterno's longtime defensive coordinator. Sandusky lauded Paterno's "high standard," his "clean competition," and his "courage to practice what he preached."

It was the height of pitiful irony, considering the words and their source.

As he offered his tribute, Sandusky was facing trial for multiple allegations of child sexual abuse over several years. When a Penn State graduate assistant told Paterno in 2002 that he had witnessed Sandusky raping a young boy in a campus shower, Paterno failed to go to law enforcement. He failed to fire Sandusky. He failed to confront Sandusky over the incident. There were others, it later became known.

When Sandusky was finally apprehended and charged, Paterno's failure to act cost him his job. With just three games left in the regular season, the Penn State board of trustees fired him. They also fired the university president.

Joe Paterno was eighty-four. Seventy-four days after being let go from the position he cherished and which had defined his life and secured his legacy, he was dead.

In a moment of moral choice, Coach Paterno—for all of his greatness—let his "high standard" down. He did not do the right thing. Instead he did nothing. He did not exercise his "courage to practice what he preached." In that moment of crisis and decision, Joe Paterno's courage failed him when he needed it most. He opted for the path of least resistance, unwilling to accept the risk of truth.

For this choice, more children would needlessly suffer the pain and humiliation that would leave scars for life.

"I wish I had done more," Paterno said sadly. Maybe he died of a broken heart.

But this was more than a regrettable end to a great career. It offered a cautionary lesson for those of us who remain.

The eighteenth-century British statesman Edmund Burke summed up a wise maxim of morality when he declared, "All that is necessary for the triumph of evil is for good men to do nothing." Of course, it is not always easy to take a moral stand. It is easier to let things go. It is less risky to look the other way. It is less costly to remain silent. It is less troublesome to conceal your convictions.

The prophet Nathan must have known all this when God told him to go to King David to confront him over his adultery with Bathsheba. After all, it was a brutal and risky time to live—especially for prophets bearing the bad news of unvarnished truth to those in power. It was a time when kings sometimes killed the messenger—quite literally. But Nathan didn't hide or beg God to be excused. Knowing the danger of honest confrontation, he went.

When David demanded to know what kind of man would rob another man of his pet lamb and slaughter it when he had so many sheep of his own, the prophet pointed his long boney figure at the king and told him:

"Thou art the man!" (2 Samuel 12:7, KJV).

> **WE LIVE IN TIMES THAT CALL FOR COURAGE AND CHOOSING.**

And Nathan didn't lose his head. Confronted boldly with his sin, King David repented.

We live in times that call for courage and choosing. Would to God that you and I may always be willing, in every circumstance that matters to him, to take our stand for what is right—without regard to cost or sacrifice.

Let us pray for that courage—and that it never fail us.

January, 2012

Chapter Eleven: Unseen Things

"He has also set eternity in the hearts of men."

ECCLESIASTES 3:11

$\mathcal{B}$irth Pangs

There's a world of worry out there.

Everywhere you look, things seem grim. Uncertainty and confusion bombard us from a thousand media centers. It doesn't seem to be getting any better—it actually looks to be getting worse.

We may not want to see it or hear it, but we can't escape it—there's no place to hide.

Afghanistan erupts into violence over the burning of Muslim holy books at an American airfield. More than thirty people are killed, including four U.S. servicemen. In Syria, thousands seek to flee the brutal crackdown that has engulfed the country in bloodshed, even as western nations condemn the vote on a new constitution as a 'farce." Iran continues its nuclear program, seemingly oblivious to efforts by the U.S. and others to stop it. There are rumors that Israel will no longer wait before it strikes first.

To the casual observer, it seems the world is going to hell in a handbasket. To those living in the midst of this cauldron of death, mayhem, and destruction, it seems already to have arrived. As one Syrian victim said from his hospital bed: "Nobody is doing anything… We need the mercy of God."

Speaking of whom, where is he? He's right where he's always been—in complete control.

His Son warned us it would be like this toward the end. The darker the world gets, the closer God moves us to the dawn of a new day and the fulfillment of his purpose through the one who will return and reign supreme over the nations.

Jesus' disciples, just like all of us, had a fascination with the future. Matthew writes that they "came to him privately and said, 'Tell us, when will all this happen? What sign will signal your return and the end of the world?'" (Matthew 24:3, NLT). Jesus then sat down on the Mount of Olives and explained to them what was ahead. He described a geopolitical landscape that seems torn from tomorrow's headlines.

"You will hear of wars and rumors of wars—but don't be alarmed. Such things must indeed happen, but that is not the end. For one nation will rise in arms against another, and one kingdom against another, and there will be famines and earthquakes in different parts of the world. But all that is only the beginning of the birth pangs" (Matthew 24:6-8, Phillips).

Birth pangs?

Yes, we are witnessing the slow death of one world, the one God made and man has corrupted, and the coming birth of a new one—created by God to exist in glorious and eternal perfection. That's the new world we'll live in. That's the exciting future God has planned for his children.

Paul told the believers in Rome:

"Against its will, all creation was subjected to God's curse. But with eager hope, the creation looks forward to the day when it will join God's children in glorious freedom from death and decay" (Romans 8:20, 21, NLT). With "eager hope," we await the dawning of a new day.

When Jesus was drawing near to his crucifixion, he told his disciples that they would see him again. He told them that their grief over his death would "suddenly turn to wonderful joy." Jesus compared it to a woman's pain in giving birth:

"When her child is born, her anguish gives way to joy because she has brought a new baby into the world. So you have sorrow now, but I will see you again; then you will rejoice and no one can rob you of that joy" (John 16:20-22, NLT).

Birth pangs.

That's what the world is experiencing. So let us look up, for our redemption—the return of the one who loves us—is drawing near. When Christ comes and when we see him and when we share with him the new heaven and the earth, then the sorrow we feel when we witness a world aflame will be turned into joy—and our joy will never end.

Jesus tells us, "Don't be alarmed." Doom will not have the final word. The very best—for which you and I were created—is still ahead.

> SOME FEAR A HOPELESS END. THE CHRISTIAN REJOICES IN AN ENDLESS HOPE.

Some fear a hopeless end. The Christian rejoices in an endless hope.

And that makes all the difference in the world.

February, 2012

✐Thief in the Night

Poor Harold Camping.

As we'd say here in Texas, "Bless his heart."

Camping, you may recall, was the aging "Judgment Day calculator" (as one reporter described him) who told the world that everything would end on May 21, 2011. The eighty-nine-year-old Christian radio station owner said that two hundred thousand Christian believers would be taken to heaven in the Rapture. He pinpointed the precise time the world would end as 5:59 p.m.

I had to give some thought to what I would tell our church the next morning if Camping's prophecy came true and we were all, so to speak, "Left Behind."

The following week, however, David Letterman, Jon Stewart, Bill Maher, and every other late-night host and public commentator who revels in the strangeness of Christians, were having an understandable field day. A good laugh—at the expense of the sacred—was had by all. Shortly after the apocalyptic dud (AKA "Apocalypse (Not) Now"), Mr. Camping explained his miscalculation as simply a slight misinterpretation of his numerical evidence. Camping insisted that Judgment Day had happened on May 21; we just didn't see it.

"We didn't see any difference, but God brought Judgment Day to bear upon the whole world," he said. "The whole world is under Judgment Day and it will continue right up until Oct. 21, 2011 and by that time the whole world will be destroyed."

Cool spin! And a new date!

It did give us all a few more months to get better prepared—and anticipate the further humorous ridicule on October 22.

> THERE WAS A SERIOUS OBSERVATION IN THIS HARMLESS ENTERTAINMENT. GOD IS GOING TO JUDGE THE WORLD SOME DAY. THAT'S A FACT. JESUS CHRIST IS GOING TO RETURN TO EARTH SOME DAY. THIS IS ALSO A FACT.

But there was a serious observation in this harmless entertainment. God is going to judge the world some day. That's a fact. Jesus Christ is going to return to earth some day. This is also a fact. And the attitude of the world toward its own demise is going to continue to be what it was following Camping's nonsense. The Scriptures are very clear about this.

Jesus tells us that "no one knows the day or hour when these things will happen, not even the angels in heaven or the Son himself. Only the Father knows" (Matthew 24:36, NLT). Of course this hasn't stopped Hal Lindsey, Harold Camping, or dozens of other self-styled end-time prophets from crying wolf. Dates have been set for hundreds of years.

But there was a day when the wolf actually showed up.

Jesus compared the situation to the days of Noah: "In those days before the flood, the people were enjoying banquets and parties and weddings right up to the time Noah entered the boat. People didn't realize what was going to happen until the flood came and swept them all away. That is the way it will be when the Son of Man comes" (Matthew 24:38, 39, NLT).

Men like Camping help to anesthetize the world to the fearful reality of God's coming judgment; they enable people to take it lightly. But the Bible advises us against that.

The apostle Paul writes: "the day of the Lord's return will come unexpectedly, like a thief in the night. When people are saying 'Everything is peaceful and secure,' then disaster will fall..." (1 Thessalonians 5:2, 3, NLT). The apostle Peter reminds us that "in the last days scoffers will come, mocking the truth and following their own desires. They will say, 'What happened to the promise that Jesus is coming again? From before the times of our ancestors, everything has remained the same since the world was first created'" (2 Peter 3:3, 4, NLT).

Some day it won't be the same. Some day the end of the world as we know it will come.

What kind of a day will it be? It will dawn like any other. Nobody will be talking about it. Nobody will be predicting it. Nobody will be laughing about it, or making jokes about it. Nobody will even be thinking about it or expecting it.

That's when it will come.

"Like a thief in the night."

June, 2011

$\mathscr{H}e$ Speaks in the Silence

Noise. There's a lot of it in our lives. With omnipresent cell phones, Blackberries, and laptops, we're more in touch and doing more communicating than ever. And we've also got more information. Silence isn't golden. It's nonexistent!

But perhaps we should re-create a bit of silence in our lives.

In 1 Kings 19, the prophet Elijah has just recently vanquished the false prophets of Baal on Mount Carmel. It's one of the most dramatic confrontations found anywhere in the Bible. God grants Elijah a total triumph. Yet in the very next chapter, we find Elijah fleeing for his life to Sinai, as despondent now as he was triumphant just a few verses before.

"I have had enough, Lord," Elijah sighs in exhaustion. "Take my life, for I am no better than my ancestors…" (I Kings 19:4, NLT). God tells Elijah to leave his cave where he is hiding out and go and "stand before me on the mountain." This Elijah does.

The Bible tells us that "the Lord passed by" in a violent and loud windstorm that ripped the rocks from the ground. But then we read something curious: "But the Lord was not in the wind." This violent storm is followed by a great earthquake, but once again we read that "the Lord was not in the earthquake." Then there was "a fire, but the Lord was not in the fire."

So, where was the Lord, if not in all this loud and boisterous activity? After all, isn't this the same mighty God who threw down flames of fire that devoured the offering as a test of faith and power in the last chapter? Yes, it is.

But this time, God spoke through "the sound of a gentle whisper. When Elijah heard it, he wrapped his face in his cloak and went out and stood at the entrance of the cave" (1 Kings 19:12, 13). And then God gave Elijah the prophet his marching orders. The King James Version describes this "gentle whisper" as "a still small voice." God did not choose to speak through all the loud cataclysms of his creation. He waited for those to pass by. Then he spoke in a soft and quiet whisper.

Are we not sometimes too distracted by noise and dramatic activity to truly hear the voice of God speaking to us? In the ceaseless pressures of life in the twenty-first century, are you and I perhaps too busy to take time to meditate and contemplate and reflect? Life is rapid mass transit. We need to make time to stop everything and pay attention to God. "Be still," he commands us through the psalmist, "and know that I am God" (Psalm 46:10, KJV).

> WE NEED TO MAKE TIME TO STOP EVERYTHING AND PAY ATTENTION TO GOD. "BE STILL," HE COMMANDS US THROUGH THE PSALMIST, "AND KNOW THAT I AM GOD." (Ps. 46:10).

When we are still, when we get off our treadmill and when we really quiet ourselves in uninterrupted meditation before his throne, we'll discover that the still, small voice we hear is God whispering to our heart his love and peace through all the earthquakes, fires, and windstorms of our lives.

March, 2009

Indra's New Digs

Indra Tamang couldn't claim it. He had no legal right to it. And he didn't see it coming. But it changed his life.

What a surprise it must have been.

Indra grew up in rural Nepal. As a child he lived in abject poverty in a mud hut. In his twenties, he decided to come to America. "I was always hearing about America," he said. "I took my chance and came." It was quite a step of faith for a young man from Nepal. Indra knew he'd never be the same. No one who comes to America ever is.

Ruth Ford gave Indra a job. For thirty years he served faithfully as her butler, cook, and caretaker. When she passed away in 2009 at the age of ninety-eight, she left Indra, her trusted servant and friend, not one but two apartments at one of the most desirable addresses in New York City: Manhattan's famed Dakota building. In addition to the two apartments, Ford also left Indra a collection of valuable Russian art.

Amazing!

The young man who seized an opportunity to change his life became a faithful servant. Years later, his employer became his benefactor and—as an act of grace and generosity—bequeathed to him an inheritance beyond his wildest dreams.

When a person gives his or her life to Jesus Christ and becomes his follower, that individual seizes an opportunity that will change his or her life forever. We live the remainder of our lives in faithful service to God and to others. Whatever we achieve and acquire of this world's goods and recognition pales in comparison to the glorious spiritual inheritance that awaits us in heaven.

> WHEN A PERSON GIVES HIS OR HER LIFE TO JESUS CHRIST AND BECOMES HIS FOLLOWER, THAT INDIVIDUAL SEIZES AN OPPORTUNITY THAT WILL CHANGE HIS OR HER LIFE FOREVER.

In his first letter, Peter describes our salvation and eternal destiny as "a priceless inheritance–an inheritance that is kept in heaven for you, pure and undefiled, beyond the reach of change and decay" (1 Peter 1:4, NLT).

This gift—this eternal bequest—has been given to us by God without regard to merit or favor on our part. We cannot earn it and we can claim no right to it. Nor, like Indra, do we stand in any natural relationship to inherit it.

God has chosen us as his children. He has adopted us into his family. Once we were estranged from God, aliens—even his enemies. But we were chosen by God to be his special children.

This is the meaning of grace.

Indra Tamang was the recipient of extravagant grace. So are we. The God who made the universe in six days has a Son who has been preparing a home for us for more than two thousand years. You could say that compared to what we have to look forward to forever, what we have now in this life is the difference between a mud hut in Nepal and an apartment in Manhattan.

The next time this old world gets you down—the next time you turn off the news and shake your weary head—think of Indra enjoying that pad in the Dakota. And then thank God for your salvation and your eternal inheritance.

And the home that is waiting for you.

May, 2010

*O*ur Eternal Spring

By the time you read this, today will be a memory, hopefully a pleasant one.

It's Tuesday, the third day of spring.

And what a beautiful day! Temperatures in the seventies, sunny, with a gentle breeze and nary a cloud in the sky.

Now that's more like it!

It wasn't anything like this when spring announced its arrival a few days ago. At least here in North Texas. Here it was anything but spring. A cloudy arctic blast had sent temperatures diving and even dropped some snow on us. I thought I was back in Maine—well, perhaps Maine in June.

Just days before, things were much more spring-like. The pear trees had sent forth their beautiful white blossoms and the grass was poking through. We had turned the corner on what had been—for us Texans—an unusually challenging winter. But now God's lovely season of change and growth was upon us. And then—wham!—we were right back in winter, just like that. And on the first day of spring, no less.

As I looked at the snow resting on the blossoms, I knew this cold wouldn't last. Everyone else knew it too. Winter would go. It had been here long enough. Spring had come. The snow would melt. The air would warm. "This too shall pass." The calendar didn't lie.

New life could not be denied.

So we toughed out one last blast. The future was bright—and it was just around the corner. So we didn't fret or worry or complain.

Whether we live in Maine or Texas, God gives us spring to remind us that there is hope ahead. That's why it's fitting that we celebrate the resurrection at this time of year. The winter of sin has howled across our civilization. It has sent hope into the single digits. It has frozen God's creation in its icy grip and the branches of justice, love, and joy sometimes seem barren.

In the resurrection of his Son, God told us that this winter would not last. If Good Friday was one last arctic blast, Easter morning was the glorious assurance that new life could not be denied.

The leaders of the church in the first century knew this.

"But thank God!" exclaimed Paul to the Corinthians. "He gives us victory over sin and death through our Lord Jesus Christ" (1 Corinthians 15:57, NLT). Paul also knew that this victory was not just the singular triumph of God's Son. It was a cosmic victory. It wasn't just God bringing Jesus in from the cold. It meant the end of winter.

Paul wrote to the Christians at Rome:

"Against its will, all creation was subjected to God's curse. But with eager hope, the creation looks forward to the day when it will join God's children in glorious freedom from death and decay" (Romans 8:20, 21, NLT).

> IN EVERY BLADE OF GRASS THAT PUSHES THROUGH THE SOIL, IN EVERY BLOSSOM THAT BLOOMS, IN EVERY LEAF THAT SPROUTS, IN EVERY NOTE OF THE SONGBIRD, YOU AND I ARE REMINDED THAT SIN AND DEATH WILL NEVER HAVE THE LAST WORD.

The whole created order will witness the end of the season of death, and join with joyful celebration in the season of new life.

In every blade of grass that pushes through the soil, in every blossom that blooms, in every leaf that sprouts, in every note of the songbird, you and I are reminded that sin and death will never have the last word.

In Jesus Christ, life conquered the grave. This is how we know that our hope will finally break into joy—forever.

This will be our eternal spring.

March, 2010

The Body Snatcher

Jean Stevens loved her sister June. They were twins.

Jean also loved her husband Jim. They were married sixty years.

When June and Jim passed away, it was more than Jean could handle. "Death is very hard for me to take," she said. At ninety-one and living alone in a ramshackle old house on a lonely country road in rural Pennsylvania, Jean had to do something to ease her grief. So she decided that June and Jim would move in with her.

After they were dead.

When Jim died, Jean had his body secretly exhumed from the local cemetery and brought home. She propped him up on a couch in a detached garage. Apparently that was close enough. But when sister June passed away ten years later, Jean had her body dug up from the backyard and brought right into a spare room off the bedroom.

Calling Norman Bates!

"I think when you put them in the [ground]," Jean softly explained, "that's good-bye, good-bye. In this way, I could touch her and look at her and talk to her." Jean took real good care of her beloved sister. She sprayed her with expensive perfume–June's favorite. "I'd go in, and I'd talk, and I'd forget," Jean told a reporter. "I put glasses on her. When I put the glasses on, it made all the difference in the world. I would fix her up. I'd fix her face up all the time." She also went out to the garage and talked to Jim, who looked pretty nifty in his dark suit, white shirt, and blue knit tie. At least for a while (he was out there for a decade).

Finally, someone tipped off the police, and they came and got June and Jim.

Jean explained that part of what motivated her to go this extreme to maintain direct contact, as it were, was her uncertainty about the hereafter. Jean said of death: "Is that the grand finale?" She admitted that when she looked at creation—the stars and the moon and the animals of the woods—she did think that perhaps there was a creator after all.

"I don't always go to church, but I want to believe," Jean said.

Still, she was mortified (sorry!) that the bodies of her loved ones would spend eternity in an underground casket. "That's suffocation to me, even though you aren't breathing," she said.

Dr. Helen Lavretsky, a professor at UCLA who has researched the subject of the elderly and death, conceded that those who aren't particularly spiritual or religious do have a more difficult time dealing with death, which they regard as final.[49]

That's natural and understandable—and so sad.

Jesus told Martha that whoever placed his or her faith in him, "would never ever die." Jesus defied death in word: "I am the resurrection and the life," he declared. Then he defied death in deed: "Jesus shouted, 'Lazarus, come out!'" And Martha's brother, Lazarus, did (John 11:25, 26; 43, NLT).

> ETERNAL LIFE: IT'S THE GREATEST DIFFERENCE; IT'S OUR GREATEST HOPE.

That was Jesus' greatest miracle. And his greatest victory? When the stone rolled away on Easter morning. The apostle Paul comforted the Corinthians:

"For we know that when this earthly tent we live in is taken down (that is, when we die and leave this body) we will have a house in heaven, an eternal body made for us by God himself and not by human hands."

Paul added:

"We grow weary in our present bodies, and we long to put on our heavenly bodies like new clothing... it's not that we want to die... rather, we want to put on our new bodies so that these dying bodies will be swallowed up by life. God himself has prepared us for this..." (2 Corinthians 5:1, 2, 4, 5, NLT).

Jean Stevens said, "I want to believe." Let's pray she does. Eternal life: it's the greatest difference; it's our greatest hope.

And it sure beats propping up corpses on a couch in the garage.

September, 2010

*T*he Carriage Ride

The last thing everyone does is the last thing most people want to do. Die.

The poet Emily Dickinson famously wrote:

"Because I could not stop for Death,
He kindly stopped for me;
The carriage held but just ourselves
And Immortality.
"We slowly drove, he knew no haste,
And I had put away
My labor, and my leisure too,
For his civility."[50]

Most of us would rather not "stop for Death." We don't even slow down. We don't think about death, we don't talk about death, and we don't much prepare for it. And so death will always stop for us—usually when we least expect the visit. We'll step into the carriage and we'll be chaperoned by Immortality out of this world. Ready or not, we'll "put away" our labor and our leisure too.

Dickinson's was but one of countless interpretations of this great universal

event. Thomas H. Johnson called death "one of the great characters of literature." Shortly after his beloved son Quentin died during World War I, Theodore Roosevelt said that "life and death are part of the same great adventure."

I've always liked that view.

The following year, Roosevelt passed away quietly in his sleep. Vice President Thomas R. Marshall commented that "death had to catch him sleeping.
If he had been awake, there would have been a fight."

One man who waged a long and courageous fight against death was the
iconic Steve Jobs. The high-tech inventor and entrepreneur who abandoned
Christianity in his youth and became a Buddhist, lost his battle with cancer
at the age of fifty-six. He once said this concerning death:

"Death is very likely the single best invention of life. Almost everything,
all external expectations, all pride, all fear of embarrassment or failure: these
things just fall away in the face of death."[51]

The Bible describes death as an appointment: "It is appointed to men once
to die" (Hebrews 9:27, KJV).

Death isn't just a definitive, transformative event—it's a scheduled one.

The last thing Jobs told his biographer Walter Isaacson was that he would
beat the cancer that had ravaged him. But even Jobs wasn't strong enough, re-
sourceful enough, or smart enough to resched-
ule his appointment with eternity. The great
business leader, like all before him, had to put
away his labor and his leisure too.

The Bible pulls no punches about the great
matters of life and death. And its wisdom is the
wisdom of God. "Lord," the psalmist writes,
"remind me how brief my time on earth will
be. Remind me that my days are numbered—
how fleeting my life is... My entire lifetime is
just a moment to you; at best, each of us is but
a breath." And then the writer, David, adds
perspective to all our plans and hopes, and our
dreams and schemes:

FOR THE PERSON
WHO HAS PLACED
HIS OR HER FAITH
IN JESUS CHRIST,
ALL FEAR OF
DEATH HAS BEEN
REMOVED. AND THIS
SPIRITUAL REALITY
HAS ENORMOUS
IMPLICATIONS.

"We are merely moving shadows, and all our
busy rushing ends in nothing" (Psalm 39:5, 6, NLT). Steve Jobs was right:
"These things just fall away in the face of death."

For the person who has placed his or her faith in Jesus Christ, all fear of death has been removed. And this spiritual reality has enormous implications. When Christ rose from the dead, his resurrection changed everything forever. For the Christian, "life and death are part of the same great adventure." Instead of being a fearsome "grim reaper," death is now a kindly and civil escort who will guide us to a new and glorious life of which this life is but the momentary prelude. We'll be happy to "put away" our labor and our leisure too.

Christians are going home. We cannot postpone the appointment. Instead, we'll welcome it. In the face of the sober truth of mortality, David rhetorically asked: "And so, Lord, where do I put my hope? My only hope is in you" (Palm 39:7, NLT).

It is more than enough. We need not fear the summons. Heaven will be opened before us.

Afraid? I can hardly wait! I'm going to hop into that carriage. It's the difference Christ makes.

November, 2011

ᴖotes

1. John Godfrey Saxe: *The Blind Men and the Elephant*, from *The Poems of John Godfrey Saxe* (Boston, MA, Houghton, Mifflin and Company), 1881.

2. Walter Isaacson: *Einstein: His Life and Universe* (New York, Simon & Schuster), 2007; Chapter 17, *Einstein's God*, pg 385.

3. Walter Isaacson: quoted in *The Scale of Einstein, From Faith to Formulas*, by Janet Maslin; The New York Times online, *Review of Books*, April 9, 2007.

4. Albert Einstein, in remarks to Rabbi Herbert Goldstein in 1929, in Isaacson: *Einstein: His Life and Universe*, pg. 385.

5. Clive Staples Lewis: *The Weight of Glory*, *"Is Theology Poetry?"* Preached originally as a sermon in the Church of St. Mary the Virgin, Oxford, on June 8, 1942; later published in *The Weight of Glory and Other Addresses*, Revised and expanded edition (New York, Macmillan), 1980.

6. Richard Attenborough, quoted in *Charles Darwin and the Tree of Life*, documentary produced by the British Broadcasting Corporation, 2009.

7. Satoshi Kanazawu, in a study published in the March, 2010 issue of *Social Psychology Quarterly*.

8. Colson made this observation on numerous public occasions, on radio and in his public speeches; other commentators and authors have used variations of this assertion to underscore the lack of spiritual depth within the Church.

9. Winston Churchill: *The Russian Enigma*, a BBC radio broadcast in London on October 1, 1939.

10. John M. Barry: *Roger Williams and the Creation of the American Soul: Church, State and the Birth of Liberty* (New York, Viking Press) 2012, quoted in a book review in *The Wall Street Journal*, December 30, 2011.

11. *"Robert Jeffress endorses Rick Perry, says Mormonism is a 'cult'"*, *The Washington Post*, October 7, 2011.

12. Martin Rinkart (1586-1649): *Now Thank We All Our God*, translated by Catherine Winkworth (1827-1878), arranged by Eldon Burkwall (1928-).

13. John R. W. Stott: *The Message of Thessalonians*, The Bible Speaks Today (Downers Grove, Ill., InterVarsity Press), 1979.

14. Mark Hatfield: Conflict and Conscience (Waco, Texas, Word Books), 1971, pg 13.

15. John R. W. Stott: *Between Two Worlds: The Art of Preaching in the Twentieth Century* (Grand Rapids, Michigan, William B. Eerdmans Publishing Company), 1982, pg. 15.

16. John Stott: *The Living Church: Convictions of a Lifelong Pastor* (Downers

Grove, Illinois, IVP Books), 2007, pg. 149.

17.[pg 100] Francis Bacon, Sr., English lawyer and philosopher (1561-1626), quoted in *The New Encyclopedia of Christian Quotations*, complied by Mark Water (Grand Rapids, MI, Baker Books, a Division of Baker Book House Co.), 2000, pg.102.

18. Rick Reilly: *I believe in Tim Tebow*; a ESPN commentary originally published on ESPN.com January 13, 2012.

19. Edward Mote (1797-1874) and William B. Bradbury (1816-1868): *The Solid Rock*; text written, 1834; music composed, 1863.

20. Richard Cobden (1804-1865), British manufacturer and Liberal statesman, is largely credited with the successful repeal of the Corn Laws in England; source unknown.

21. George Matheson (1842-1906), *Inspiring Quotations: Contemporary & Classical*, complied by Albert Wells, Jr.(Nashville, TN, Thomas Nelson, Inc.), 1988, pg. 153.

22. Robert D. Putnam and David E. Campbell: *American Grace: How Religion Divides and Unites Us* (New York, Simon & Schuster), 2010.

23. Rob Dreher: *All American Grace,* published as an Op - Ed in The Dallas Morning News, November 28, 2010.

24. Christian Smith and Melissa Lundquist Denton: *Soul Searching: The Religious and Spiritual Lives of American Teenagers* (New York, Oxford University Press, Inc.), 2005.

25. Damon Linker: *The Future of Christian America*, in The New Republic, April 7, 2009.

26. G.K. Chesterton: essay entitled Christmas, in *All Things Considered*, originally published in 1908; public domain.

27. C. S. Lewis: *The Problem of Pain* (New York, Macmillan), 1962.

28. Rob Bell: *Love Wins: A Book About Heaven, Hell and the Fate of Every Person Who Ever Lived* (New York, Harper Collins), 2011.

29. Dr. R. Albert Mohler, Jr: *We Have Seen All This Before: Rob Bell and the (Re) Emergence of Liberal Theology* on *AlbertMohler.com.*, March 16, 2011.

30. Richard Niebuhr: *The Kingdom of God in America* (New York, Harper & Row Publishers, Inc.), 1937.

31. Charles Krauthammer: *Don't Touch My Junk*, in an Op-Ed in *The Washington Post*, November 19, 2010.

32. Philip Yancey: *Prayer: Does It Make Any Difference?* (Grand Rapids, Michigan, Zondervan), 2006,pg. 41.

33. C.S. Lewis: *Malcolm*, quoted in Yancey: *Prayer: Does It Make Any Difference?*, pg. 42.

34. Patti Davis: *Angels Don't Die: My Father's Gift of Faith* (New York, Harper Collins Publishers), 1995.

35. Watchman Nee (1903-1972), Chinese Christian author and church leader, *Inspiring Quotations: Contemporary & Classical*, complied by Albert Wells, Jr.(Nashville, TN, Thomas Nelson, Inc.), 1988, pg. 30.

36. Cathy Lynn Grossman: *As Protestants decline, those with no religion gain*, published in *USA Today*, October 9, 2012.

37. *ibid*

38. C.S. Lewis, *"Christian Apologetics"* (1945) included in *God in the Dock* (Grand Rapids, MI, William B.Eerdmans Publishing Co.),1970, pg.101-102.

39. William Butler Yeats (1865-1939):*The Second Coming*, written in 1919 in the aftermath of the first World War, published in the edition of *Michael Robartes and the Dancer*,1920; public domain.

40. Matt Chandler: *Words of Life: The Only Place of Hope*, adapted from a sermon entitled *Divine Tensions*, May, 2010.

41. *Ibid*.

42. *Ibid*.

43. William Sloan Coffin (1924-2006): Alex's Death, from *The Courage to Love* by William Sloan Coffin (New York, Harper Collins Publishing, Inc) 1982, reprinted in *A Chorus of Witnesses: Model Sermons for Today's Preacher*, edited by Thomas G. Long & Cornelius Plantinga, Jr. (Grand Rapids, William B. Eeerdmans Publishing Co.)1994, pg. 262.

44. Philip Yancey makes this argument in his book *Rumors of Another World: What on Earth Are We Missing?* (Grand Rapids, MI, Zondervan), 2003.

45. *The Story of my dissolute, lonely, useless young life (and why it was the making of me) by Sir Anthony Hopkins*, in an interview by Elaine Lipworth, *The Daily Mail*, London, March 1, 2010.

46. Christopher Hitchens: *When the King Saved God; Vanity Fair*, May, 2011.

47. C.S. Lewis: *A Grief Observed*, originally published under the pseudonym N.W. Clerk (London, Faber & Faber), 1961; re-published under Lewis' name in 1963, following his death.

48. James Russell Lowell (1819-1891): *Once to Every Man and Nation*, published in *The Boston Courier* on December 11, 1845 in protest to America's war with Mexico; later set to music as a hymn.

49. *Pa. widow lives with corpses of her husband and twin sister*, by Michael Rubinkam, The Associated Press, *The Bangor Daily News*, Bangor, Maine, July 6, 2010, pg 1.

50. Emily Dickinson (1830-1886): Because I could not stop for Death, published posthumously in 1890 in a collection called *Poems: Series 1*.

51. Steve Jobs: Commencement Address to Stanford University, June 2005. This moving speech was delivered shortly after Jobs underwent surgery for pancreatic cancer.

About the Author

Jack Wyman has spent more than thirty-five years in Christian ministry and public life. As a local school board member, state lawmaker, lobbyist and twice a candidate for statewide office, he has put his faith to the test in the political arena. As a popular college professor and presidential historian, he has inspired young people to appreciate the uniqueness of the American experience. And as a pastor and preacher, Wyman has encouraged believers to embrace the exciting intersection of their Christian faith and this turbulent world.

Jack Wyman has accepted theologian Karl Barth's challenge to "preach with the Bible in one hand and a newspaper in the other."

It is his conviction that Christianity impacts all of life that leads Wyman to encourage true followers of Jesus Christ to accept and live out a fully integrated faith.

A native New Englander, Wyman holds a BA degree in History and a Master's in Political Science from the University of Maine. He served as executive director of the Christian Civic League of Maine for a decade, and for another ten years held various positions within Prison Fellowship Ministries. He has served as the pastor of four churches in Maine, Connecticut and Texas. Wyman and his wife Elisabeth have three grown daughters and two grandchildren. They make their home in Highland Village, Texas.